D0219003

Business Research Projects

Business Research Projects:

A solution-oriented approach

Jimme A. Keizer

Piet M. Kempen

AMSTERDAM • BOSTON • HEIDELBERG • LONDON • NEW YORK
OXFORD • PARIS • SAN DIEGO • SAN FRANCISCO
SINGAPORE • SYDNEY • TOKYO

Butterworth-Heinemann is an imprint of Elsevier

ELSEVIER

BH

Butterworth-Heinemann is an imprint of Elsevier
Linacre House, Jordan Hill, Oxford OX2 8DP
30 Corporate Drive, Suite 400, Burlington, MA 01803

First published 2006

British Library Cataloguing in Publication Data
A catalogue record for this book is available from the British Library

Library of Congress Cataloguing in Publication Data
A catalogue record for this book is available from the Library of Congress

ISBN-13: 978-0-7506-6573-5
ISBN-10: 0-7506-6573-4

For information on all Butterworth-Heinemann publications
visit our web site at http://books.elsevier.com

Printed and bound in Great Britain

06 07 08 09 10   10 9 8 7 6 5 4 3 2 1

Working together to grow
libraries in developing countries

www.elsevier.com | www.bookaid.org | www.sabre.org

ELSEVIER   BOOK AID International   Sabre Foundation

Contents

Preface

Almost all higher educational institutions have built some kind of fieldwork project into the advanced stages of their programmes. This reflects a development in which final qualifications in higher education have been moving from being solely knowledge oriented towards criteria integrating both theory and practice, and knowledge and skills.

At the end of their formal higher education students should be able to apply their acquired knowledge and understanding in a manner that indicates a professional approach to their work or vocation, and have the ability to integrate knowledge and handle complexity, and formulate judgements with incomplete or limited information. And one may expect that they can communicate their conclusions, and the knowledge and rationale underpinning these, clearly and unambiguously to specialist and non-specialist audiences.

Opportunities for students to apply theory to practice are often limited to cases provided by textbooks or teachers in plenary or group sessions. These cases are very useful, they demonstrate the relevance of theories and models, but their often stylized form inevitably underscores the complexity of the reality in organizations. An operations management problem regarding the required minimal amount of goods a business unit should have in stock is theoretically readily solvable. Experts in this field know formulae and parameters for such problems, and students learn to use these formulae. But the stylized cases can only provide a minimal introduction to the complexities directly associated with the problem. Reality almost always presents issues like: How reliable are the available data? What if, for some parameters in the formula, there are no data available? Fieldwork projects provide an experience of reality, giving students the chance to learn and to show that they have mastered the intended qualifications. Most academically educated professionals who have undertaken a fieldwork project have a lifelong memory of their experiences in this domain of their education.

The quality of such projects is a matter of constant concern to students, teachers and managers. Students have concerns about finding an attractive and challenging project and worry about getting sufficient support and supervision from tutors as well as company coaches. Supervisors of students doing fieldwork projects want to be sure that their students realize the intended objectives and are keen to monitor their students' progress during the project. Managers from the participating organizations expect clear benefits from the results of the projects. Moreover, management is sometimes interested to discover whether a student has potential and deserves to get a job offer after the fieldwork project has been successfully completed.

This practical guide addresses the quality issues by offering the reader a comprehensive framework for going through the successive process steps of the fieldwork project. A logbook is included as an insert, which provides a checklist for each of the ten steps, enabling students to document the progress of their projects and communicate with their coaches and supervisors about the project.

Our starting point is that students, teachers and managers should have greater ambition than only delivering glossy final reports. Our opinion is that fieldwork assignments are effective if a student of a given management problem succeeds in systematically developing a solution that is adopted and implemented by management. Good assignments encourage students to deploy business and organizational theories, methods and models to contribute to the solution of real problems. Our concept of effective fieldwork is built on three basic propositions:

1 The implementation of the developed solution is part of the project
2 The early stages are critical to the success of the project
3 Support and acceptance from the case study company of the method and solution are decisive for the end result of the project.

We are convinced that content knowledge – for example, about marketing, operations management, production, strategy, information technology, facilities management, healthcare technology management, human resource management, innovation management, etc. – required to find solutions for practical problems is not the problem; it is available at a sufficient level in the respective educational institutions. The problem is that many students lack the adequate process knowledge and skills to fully exploit their content knowledge.

For the successful accomplishment of such projects, specific process knowledge and skills are required, such as:

- Recognition and description of an organizational problem
- Design and organization of a research project
- Communication with people on different levels within the organization
- Interviewing, listening, negotiating, giving presentations, persuading people
- Project management
- Developing solutions in collaboration with people in the organization
- Implementation of accepted solutions.

The aim of this book is to help students and their supervisors find their way through the complex and often hectic circumstances within which fieldwork projects are carried out, by making the most important process conditions contribute to the success of these projects.

The specific contribution of this book is in:

- highlighting, within a framework for the entire process, the critical early stages of fieldwork projects
- combining the knowledge and skills required for effective fieldwork projects
- integrating insights from both management consulting and project management in an approach to fieldwork projects
- providing principles and practical guidelines for effective fieldwork projects
- supporting students in carrying out fieldwork projects individually

■ challenging students to probe the initial formulation of the problem and to concentrate on finding academically and professionally high-quality implementable solutions.

We hope that, for the readers of this book, fieldwork projects will be a great learning experience, contributing to a satisfactory completion of their studies, but also beneficial to their personal and professional development.

Jimme A. Keizer

Piet M. Kempen

About the authors

Prof. Dr Piet M. Kempen studied economics and accountancy at Erasmus University, Rotterdam, and organizational science at the SIOO Inter-University Centre. After obtaining his doctorate in 1979 with the thesis 'Company diagnosis alias management audit', he became part-time professor at Eindhoven University of Technology in 1984 for the chair of Organizational Consultancy Processes (15 years). In this capacity, he worked with Dr Jimme A. Keizer to develop the Ten-Step Plan (TSP) for improving field-work and graduation projects, and put this into practice himself as fieldwork supervisor.

In the professional field, he was successively ICT advisor to Philips (three years), partner in and founder of the consultancy bureau for Van Dien & Co accountants (20 years), and director of Philips Corporate O & E (five years). He was responsible for setting up Philips's Lighthouse Consulting Group and making this independent, and has worked since 1994 as an independent consultant and trainer, with customers including educational establishments who wish to introduce the TSP. (pkempen@iae.nl)

Dr Jimme A. Keizer studied labour and organizational psychology at the University of Groningen. He worked as an organizational consultant in the non-profit sector and obtained his doctorate in 1988 after a study of the labour motivation and work satisfaction of professionals.

Since 1989, he has worked for the Organizational Science and Marketing capacity group of the Technology Management Faculty of the Technical University of Eindhoven. He is a Fellow of the Eindhoven Centre of Innovation Studies (ECIS), teaches students taking bachelor and master courses, carries out research in the field of product development in technology-intensive organizations, supervises students during fieldwork and graduation projects, and contributes to postgraduate courses. The subjects of his published work include risks in product innovation, the determinants of innovative achievements, the learning organization and facility management.

He is regularly involved in providing training and consultancy for educational establishments who wish to include the Ten-Step Plan in their practical projects.
(j.a.keizer@tue.nl)

Part 1

Model of a fieldwork project

In this book we start from the assumption that students carrying out fieldwork assignments wish to achieve more than delivering a glossy final report that is never used. The basic principle of this book is that fieldwork assignments are effective if students succeed in systematically developing a solution that is adopted and implemented by management. Good assignments encourage students to deploy theories, methods and models to contribute to the solution of real problems. In practice, it does not seem to be easy for students to work in a manner such that the business organization can implement their results at the end of the project.

As a point of departure for developing an approach that leads to more effective fieldwork, we consider the fieldwork project as a management consulting project in which the company acts as principal and the student as consultant.

- The company formulates an assignment
- The student studies the causes and backgrounds, develops proposals and contributes to the implementation of these proposals.

This point of departure implies that we use the thoughts and actions of management consultants as a reference for students. The question we want to answer is what students in their role as consultant need to do to make their project successful.

Part 1 outlines the approach used in this book to carry out a fieldwork assignment in the form of a consulting process. It starts by listing seven requirements that such a consulting process must meet to be successful.

We subsequently present a model of the assignment process that takes these requirements into account. This approach to the overall consulting strategy comprises three phases: the orientation phase, the research and solution phase, and the implementation phase. Within these phases, ten consecutive steps can be distinguished.

The main characteristics of this model for effective fieldwork assignments are:

- Implementation forms an explicit part of the fieldwork project
- Much attention is paid to the start of the project – the first phase comprises no less than six of the ten steps
- Much attention is paid to obtaining support for the solution that will be developed.

Chapter 1

The fieldwork project as a consulting process

Graduating and consultancy

The final stage of many programmes in higher vocational and university education is a fieldwork project. In such projects, students are asked to put into practice what they have learned by solving a specific organizational problem. To successfully carry out a fieldwork project one needs to have a number of skills, being able to:

- Recognize and describe a problem
- Organize the research
- Communicate with people from different levels in the organization
- Hold interviews, give presentations, listen to, negotiate with and convince people
- Independently set up a fieldwork project and carry it out according to plan
- Come up with solutions in co-operation with people from the organization
- Implement the accepted solutions.

These skills resemble the skills management consultants must possess to be able to carry out their work successfully. Consultants are faced with the task of introducing improvements in organizations where they have no authority. They cannot take decisions and give instructions themselves, since this is the domain of management. A consultant's contribution will only be effective if he or she is able to arouse interest in tackling a point for improvement in the right way at the right time. How things can go wrong is illustrated in the following case.

Case 1.1

The chair of the board of directors of an industrial concern called in a consultant who was recommended to him by a good business friend. The consultant was called in because a discussion had arisen in the concern's management about one of the subsidiaries. The topic of the discussion was whether or not the subsidiary should be sold. The consultant told the chair that he would need a few days to work on the assignment. This surprised the chair, since he and his staff had been wrestling with this problem for months, but he did not say anything about this to the consultant. Two weeks later he had another meeting with the consultant, who handed him a four-page report advising him to sell the subsidiary. The consultant also suggested a selling price. The chair and his staff were baffled by such a short report. When they asked him whether he had actually visited the subsidiary to interview people there, the consultant replied that such a visit was unnecessary as he had been able to find all necessary financial data in directly accessible sources of information. He explained that the subsidiary was too small to stand up to its competition and that it would be impossible to ever recover the capital required to obtain a better market position. The chair and his board of directors disregarded the advice and decided not to sell the subsidiary. Three years later – after heavy losses – they finally did sell, for half the price the consultant had suggested earlier. In a frank interview the chair later said: 'The consultant was right, but we did not follow his advice because he had not done enough "preliminary work" and had not entered into discussions with our people.'

This case illustrates that effective advice needs more than a well-written report.

The position students find themselves in has much in common with that of professional management consultants. Like consultants, they enter a company or institution to help realize an organizational change. Both do research and come up with a solution for which they have to find a willing ear within the company. Both will only be successful if their work not only results in a report, but also in the decision to actually implement the solution. This, of course, requires knowledge, knowledge that is available in an educational course – for instance, knowledge on marketing, production, data processing, logistics and strategy. Besides knowledge, the ability to deal with *consultative* situations is of the utmost importance. This book deals particularly with this 'skill'. To that end, we look frequently at the functioning of professional management consultants. This offers not only possibilities, but also limitations. The *skills* that are needed in the consulting profession in particular require a certain aptitude. One person may find it difficult to carry out an orderly interview, even though he or she is familiar with all the textbooks on the subject, while another may find conducting interviews in an orderly manner comes naturally. Some additional training can work miracles.

In this book, (future) fieldwork students are provided with the tools to carry out fieldwork projects effectively. For this purpose, the consulting process is described by means of a model that is based on our actual experience from consulting practice.[1] The use of this model is facilitated by the following:

- The fieldwork project is divided into ten steps (Ten-Step Plan, TSP)
- A step-by-step description of the necessary activities and the desired/intended end product is provided
- A checklist is given at the end of each step, to determine whether the intended objective of this step has been achieved
- A number of small cases are included to help put the knowledge acquired in this book into practice.

The TSP is discussed from the perspective of a professional consultant as much as possible – for instance, by means of short descriptions of actual cases, which reflect our experience in supervising students in fieldwork projects.

However, before we focus on the description of the TSP model, we first explain what we understand to be *effective consulting* – as well as an effective fieldwork project. If one is satisfied with a good report as a final product, like the consultant's report in Case 1.1, having a thorough command of professional knowledge and skills will largely suffice. However, if students want to include the acceptance and practical implementation of advice in their consulting and/or fieldwork projects, consulting skills then play an important role.

We have opted for the second approach and will therefore first examine what we consider to be effective consulting.

Effective consulting

In our view, effective consulting is the systematic development of recommended advice that is subsequently adopted and implemented by the company to which the advice is given.

Too many consulting reports, particularly those produced by students, are not used by companies. Nevertheless, students are graduating on the basis of such never-used reports. Obviously, effectiveness is not an important assessment criterion for teachers, who may settle for a performance that, in hindsight, appears to be of no use to the host company.

For this reason we will pay particular attention to the question of how the practical use of fieldwork projects can be increased. This is important to the companies and institutions where students carry out their fieldwork projects, but is of even more importance to the students themselves. Learning to give *effective* advice during the educational process gives students the confidence to take this through into their first job. Employers prefer employees who can start to work in a result-oriented manner immediately. It saves training time, which is very important in a time of fierce competition.

The question is how to achieve effective advice. How can one ensure that one's fieldwork produces more than a good final report that disappears unread and unused into a filing cabinet? To accomplish this, an approach that meets the following seven criteria is necessary:

1 It should be problem directed
2 It should be environment directed
3 It should be change directed
4 Open contracting is preferable
5 Conscious positioning is required
6 It should be coherent
7 It should contain state-of-the-art knowledge.

These seven requirements are the building blocks for the TSP, which is described in this book as a guide to effective graduation projects.

Problem directed

The more urgent a problem is in a company, the more people within that company will be willing to make time to work on a solution. If profit margins are decreasing, people will be interested in advice on lowering the stock costs.

In such situations, management's interest in realizing non-mandatory environmental targets will be put on the back-burner. A student who is given the assignment to work out the stock cost issue will therefore have a better chance that his or her advice will be adopted than the student working on the environmental issue, no matter how interesting and relevant the environmental issues may be.

In this respect, students are vulnerable. They offer to take on an assignment because they have to carry out a fieldwork project. Companies are ever willing to come up with a problem to pose to students. Usually, professional consultants encounter a much more favourable scenario when asked for their help.

Aware of their starting position, students should be selective in accepting a project assignment. Before they start to work on the project, the urgency of the problem[2] and the chances of success should be considered. This does not imply that, in a situation of decreasing margins, an environmental issue is principally unattractive. During the initial orientation, a student could conclude that better energy control could lead to substantial cost savings. Thus, a student is sometimes also able to raise the level of urgency of the problem, thereby making the project more attractive and creating a relevant fieldwork project.

External orientation

Most internal company problems have external causes, relating to the competitive environment in which companies are working. In this environment there will be leaders and stragglers. To become and remain part of the leader group – or at least maintain contact with the 'midfield' companies – the company's own competitive position requires continuous efforts. Indicators on which companies can benchmark are:

- High turnover and profit
- Low costs
- High customer orientation

- Good service
- High delivery reliability
- Low stocks
- Little scrap
- High and positive reputation
- Customer-oriented products and services.

These are some indicators a company can use to compare itself with its competitors. If a company remains behind, sooner or later it will become necessary to actively secure or enhance its market position by means of internal improvement activities.

In the past, not-for-profit and governmental organizations did not have this competition. Due to various developments in the social sphere, many of them are now also susceptible to the pressures of market forces. Examples of new 'competition' are:

- Universities and colleges are competing, not only amongst themselves but also together, to maintain their number of students
- Broadcasting corporations are competing for ratings
- Utility companies are beginning to experience mutual competition
- Internal service departments in large companies are threatened with closure if their price/performance ratio is not in line with the market
- Ministries are giving up tasks if these have been superseded by developments on the free market.

The increasing competition is important for both the professional consultant and the consulting student, since assignments that may affect a company's market position have greater prospects for success (see Case 1.2).

Case 1.2

A student obtained an assignment from a wholesale company in office furniture to improve its delivery reliability. She proposed to conduct a survey first among some current and former customers. This would enable her to better estimate which services customers demanded from the company. The research showed that, compared to its competition, the company was already performing very well as regards delivery reliability, and that customers were very satisfied in that respect. However, they appeared to be very dissatisfied with the quality of the product after several years of use. The repair service left much to be desired. When reporting her findings to the assignment principal, it soon became clear that the company would profit much more from research into its product quality and service. She thus obtained a high-quality assignment.

Early insight into market and branch developments is essential to get a fieldwork project connected to a company's external challenges. Therefore, an effective consulting project should *always* start – even before the intake meeting with the assignment principal – with an external orientation.[3] This orientation will provide insights that help to:

- Negotiate the assignment successfully. A potential assignment principal is always pleasantly surprised if the student already has some insights into the market and some knowledge of the (technical) jargon.
- Get an appropriate assignment formulation, so one is not fully dependent on the input of the assignment principal. One should also be able to contribute critically to an assignment formulation focusing on concrete improvements in the company's market position.
- Focus on solutions not of an internal cosmetic nature but directly contributing to the competitive position of the company.

Change directed

If a student wants to get his or her advice accepted and implemented, special measures need to be taken from the very start of the project. What these measures are becomes clear if we look at the end situation, where a student has given his or her advice (report). In the report, the research, findings and options for solving the problem are described. If the consultant or student has worked on the report in isolation for months, there is a risk that few people, if any, in the company will be enthusiastic. If the intention is to motivate managers and staff for an organizational change, it should become their idea as well. They must feel that it is their challenge to do better and that this will be acknowledged if they succeed. If the student fails to evoke feelings of commitment and support during the project, the chances that the proposals will be implemented will decrease considerably.[4] Case 1.1 shows how things can go wrong for a professional consultant. This can also happen to students doing fieldwork assignments (see Case 1.3).

Case 1.3

Recently a student doing a fieldwork project reported his findings from interviews about customer complaints to the assignment principal. His conclusions were seriously questioned. The student therefore suggested interviewing some other customers in the presence of a member of staff. When the results confirmed earlier findings, the company was immediately prepared to take action.

This 'not-invented-here' effect should not be underestimated. A firm rule for students should therefore be that research and reporting are carried out in close co-operation with the people within the company who have responsibility for the potential implementation of the findings.

Readiness to change requires attention from the very start of the project, i.e. the formulation of the assignment and the choices regarding the design of the research. Many organizations tend to neglect the aspects of commitment and collaboration, especially when it concerns work that is carried out by students. They find it easier to let the student start with the job agreed on, so they themselves can pay attention to affairs in hand: 'We will see whether you find something interesting and useful to us.' Such projects produce reams of paper, few changes in organizations and few learning experiences for future professionals.

Open contracting

Open contracting follows naturally from a change-oriented approach. The formulation of the assignment and the plan of action should best be arranged in close collaboration with the people who will bear responsibility for bringing about the intended improvements. If one wants to involve a student in the development of a strategic plan, then not only the manager but also the entire management team should be in agreement. If the productivity of a business unit is to be increased, contracting with only the unit management is a weak start for a successful change process. It is crucial to involve not just the person who has final responsibility. It is increasingly acknowledged among managers that people who will bear the consequences of organizational change should be involved from the outset, as in the formulation of the assignment. Thus, the essential involvement is created. Right from the start, this is an important point of interest for students (see Case 1.4).

Case 1.4

In a government organization, dissatisfaction had arisen in large sections of staff about the functioning of the HR manager. This dissatisfaction had even reached the point where the Employee Council insisted that management should have an external consultant examine the efficiency of personnel management. In the end, management agreed, albeit very reluctantly, because it could only partly refute the Employee Council's criticism.

The consultant who had been approached felt that he could very well find himself in an explosive situation given the diversity of expectations. The Employee Council wanted the HR manager to be put firmly in his place. Management expected support for the personnel policy pursued by the HR manager. Following a number of interviews with the parties involved, carried out before the assignment was accepted, the consultant realized that it would not do the organization any good if 'yellow cards' were shown. This would only intensify discussions. He therefore proposed to concentrate on improvement in the communication of personnel policy to be pursued in future, based on lessons learned in the past.

If this approach is not followed, the chances are that the people involved, intentionally or not, follow the consulting project with various hidden agendas. These will then become clear during the course of the project. While one person may be very satisfied with the way things are going, another one, on the contrary, may be very concerned. If these differences of opinion and expectations continue to exist, it may stagnate the consulting project. Such a hindrance will often also decrease the willingness to accept the advice, leading to a non-effective final report.

For these reasons – involvement and risk of stagnation – it is recommended to try to neutralize possible differences at the start of the project.[5] The best way to do so is to consult the people involved early on, in the contracting phase. However, even then there is still the chance that differing views arise that need to be reconciled. Nevertheless, it still remains important to have a broadly supported assignment formulation so any differences of opinion can be settled and to keep the selected option open for discussion.

Of course, open contracting is only possible if the student is allowed a role in contracting. This is not so much a problem if the student acquires the project him- or herself. However, in some educational institutions, a third party – for example, a fieldwork project co-ordinator – may assign fieldwork assignments. In such cases, it is recommended that the student involved requests permission to have a critical look at the contract that has been agreed.[6] This principle will be discussed in Part 2.

Positioning

In any organization, an external consultant usually attracts attention, like a doctor visiting a patient at home. There is a problem in that it may be perceived that the company cannot cope on its own. The consultant is going to interfere but one does not know what to expect. This often causes feelings of discomfort and uncertainty. What will it bring the individual staff members: improvement, a step backwards or nothing at all? For these reasons, many staff members like to meet the consultant to make their visions clear so he or she can take them into consideration.

For a consultant it is important to attract attention. It underlines the relevance of the work and, since any organizational change always competes with day-to-day routines, attention also means authority and the power to make changes.[7]

Some of the consultant's 'news value' also radiates on the student. Generally, the impact of a student doing a fieldwork project is lower than that of a professional consultant. Fieldwork projects are usually less prominent for the organization, although the phenomenon described for the professional consultant unmistakably also occurs for students doing fieldwork projects. To be successful, students must ensure that their project attracts the necessary attention. After all, the objective of a fieldwork project is to come to a solution that can be implemented and to achieve some organizational change.

Intentionally or not, some students tend to behave inconspicuously and modestly. They do not want to be a bother to anybody, sometimes to the extent that very few people know who they are. It is better to regard the expectations of the company as an opportunity, a possibility to succeed and a good exercise for the future. However, students need to seek the best possible position deliberately. This means:

- Making the first contact as high up in the organization as possible
- Getting in touch with the managers who will be responsible for the intended research course
- Asking for an internal company coach with sufficient influence to make decisions and stimulate decision-making
- Increasing internal publicity about the person, the project and its importance to the company
- Periodically giving presentations to the management team on the project and its progress, outcomes and perspectives
- Maintaining neutrality and objectivity – not following one stream within the organization but concentrating on facts and findings
- Involving members of the organization in the project in order to benefit from existing knowledge and increase support for the recommendations that are being developed
- Working continuously in terms of good communication about the project within the organization.

It often occurs that organizations offer jobs to students who carried out good fieldwork projects in terms of content and process, and managed to obtain and maintain a strong consulting position. Also, students are asked to stay at the organization for a certain period after graduation, to support the completion of the project.

Coherent approach

One of the causes of problems remaining unsolved in organizations is lack of attention. A manager may consider a decline in turnover, a peak in costs or an increasing number of customer complaints as problems that are only temporary and will blow over. Sometimes this is right, sometimes it is not. In the latter case, these difficulties are symptoms of deeper-seated and more serious problems, perhaps requiring outside help from a consultant or student. The consultant's task is first to ensure that the problem receives the attention it needs but has not yet been given due to everyday pressures of work. This requires a particular approach and a focus on logical project management steps in the solution of the problem as it has been formulated.[8] To keep the organization focused and working on the fundamental solution of the problem, one step should logically follow another. Case 1.5 shows how this should *not* be done.

Case 1.5

For his fieldwork project, a student went to work for a company making accessory equipment for computers. Due to the long and unreliable supply lines for parts from low-wage countries, the company was faced with high, partly unmarketable, parts stock and low supply reliability. Although the product's market position was still strong, the company started to lose customers. The student started to vigorously analyse the problem. He was focusing so much on quick results that he started to deal with all kinds of minor problems, losing sight of the main problem. When his fieldwork project was finished, he had indeed created a more convenient layout for the order forms, arranged the stockroom in a more orderly manner and set up a well-organized customer database, but the problem which he was taken on to address had not been solved.

He had adapted himself extremely well to the company's culture of 'putting out small fires'.

Professional consultants attain focused attention by developing a tight timeframe in which to develop a solution – after a good initial orientation on the problem – and guiding the company within this timeframe. They apply project management principles by determining throughput times and intermediary feedback sessions. Work groups are formed that receive clear tasks, and the outputs of such teams are linked together from one step to the next. They challenge management to make time for delivering the required information and making the necessary decisions. Thus, the project is lifted above the daily routine and the utmost is done to achieve an effective solution and implementation process.

State-of-the-art knowledge

Of course, in a fieldwork project, a student should apply high-level knowledge. It marks the end of studies and the transition to a professional career. At the end of the project, the student is always subjected to an examination about the process and content of the project. One of the questions asked is often whether the student has designed and carried out the project in accordance with state-of-the-art knowledge. Has he or she shown the ability to apply the theories, concepts, methods and models learned during the study, not only in a conventional way but also creatively? In our experience, the development of academic content is strongly correlated with the ability to control the TSP elements of process conditions. Together, they determine the quality of the end result. The TSP approach creates conditions in which the project can be developed from start to finish.

Ten-Step Plan (TSP)

Based on the seven design requirements described above, we have developed a model for the assignment process, depicted in Figure 2.1[9](p. 21). The entire process is divided into three successive phases:

1   *Orientation phase* – during which an external and internal exploration of the problem is carried out and a contract is made between the student who will do the fieldwork project and the organization involved (15 per cent of the time available for the project).
2   *Research and solution phase* – during which the actual research is carried out and adequate solutions are proposed (50 per cent).
3   *Implementation phase* – during which the adopted solutions are implemented (35 per cent).

Within these phases ten consecutive steps are distinguished. For many students, working with the TSP is not an easy task.

In practice, it appears that in many fieldwork projects the implementation phase often gets the rough end of the stick. In quite a few cases this phase is not scheduled at all; in others, there is not enough time to carry out the implementation. In principle, the implementation phase must be regarded as an indispensable part of a fieldwork project. Once students have become full-time professionals, they will be judged on their ability to contribute to achievable changes within organizations. This should be sufficient reason for teachers and students to incorporate mastering of implementation skills into the study curriculum. An important factor here is deciding on the maximum amount of time that can be spent on each phase, as indicated above.

However, there are more difficulties. During the fieldwork project incidents occur that disrupt the consulting process agreed on. For instance:

- Sudden loss of urgency of the problem to be dealt with
- The research may be much more, or much less, intensive than originally agreed
- Another activity suddenly requires attention
- A transfer of a manager who is important for the research
- The relevant people have insufficient time to co-operate with the research
- Cancellation of appointments for interviews, intermediate reporting and so on.

The experienced consultant will be familiar with the capriciousness of the consultancy practice and will have learned to deal with it. For students doing fieldwork projects it is difficult to find the balance between flexibility (following developments) and perseverance (defending and safeguarding the plotted course). One thing is clear: swimming with the tide will seldom result in an effective fieldwork project. Besides, in almost all cases there appears to be some margin for negotiations to safeguard the progress of the project, as illustrated in Case 1.6.

Case 1.6

Within the scope of her graduation project, a student carried out market research among a selected number of customers of the company where she was doing her project. The student set up the questionnaire she wanted to use in the customer interviews and presented it to management. Management was very upset about this part of the research. Although they still regarded the research as important, they were afraid to let the student deal with their customers, despite all the safety measures she proposed.

In the end, the student's offer to have the company's representatives do the interviews was accepted. The student gave some brief interview training to the representatives and thus she still managed to obtain the desired information.

Within the framework of the TSP, a number of guidelines are offered in this book to support students in their fieldwork projects:

- For each step the work that needs to be carried out is described
- For each step a checklist is given to determine whether necessary results have been obtained to be able to successfully start the subsequent step
- For each step some small cases have been incorporated for individual study
- A *Logbook* is included as an insert, based on the checklists, in which the results of the student's own fieldwork project can be recorded in due course.

For the sake of completeness, we once again state that the TSP model and all that goes with it are intended for fieldwork projects aimed at problem-solving. Useful ideas and opinions may be extracted from this book for research projects or walk-along projects, but that is not the main objective here.

Chapter notes

[1] See Gundry and Buchko (1996) for a similar approach. They describe fieldwork for small and start-up businesses, and offer many useful tips. Their step-by-step plan is less detailed than the TSP.

[2] The concept 'problem' in a fieldwork or organizational consultancy project almost always relates to a performance problem somewhere within the organization involved. It is always

subjective, as it is a question of the difference between the perceived reality and the desired reality. When we talk of a 'problem', we must make clear at the same time who has the problem, and for analysis and change, we must understand the situation as experienced by the various members of the organization. The requirements for analysis and improvement are derived from these perceptions. For the development and formulation of a problem definition in a consultancy project, see also: D.F. Togo, in Barcus and Wilkinson (1996: 10/3).

[3] Kubr (2002) also points out the importance of external orientation in organizational consultancy work. He presents a checklist for the analysis of external factors.

[4] In many publications on change processes and organizational consultancy work, the change-directed part follows the analytical part. This creates the impression that a diagnosis is carried out first and that the change does not come until afterwards. This separation of thoughts and actions is strongly discouraged. It will be difficult to make people who were not involved in the analysis enthusiastic about the implementation (see Greiner and Metzger, 1983: 269; Lippitt and Lippitt, 1994: 18 and 19; Greiner and Poulfelt, 2004). Swieringa and Wierdsma (1992) attempted to eliminate this separation between thoughts and actions. In their book on the learning organization, they emphasize this by observing that a change process is not complete until the behaviour of the members of the organization has changed. To achieve this, the learning process (read: change process) must involve thinking about and working on changing views, ideas and actions right from the start. Harvey and Brown (2005) give many useful change-directed tips.

[5] Greiner and Metzger (1983: 257) distinguished between two questions that consultants should ask themselves during the first phase of the assignment. Firstly, is the person I first made contact with the person who can act as my principal? Secondly, is the problem described to me the real problem? An evaluation of both questions is necessary; see also Tjosvold (1991), who describes how differences of opinion can be put to positive use.

[6] Open contracting as a prerequisite for professional action touches on the code of conduct for the consultant. Greiner and Metzger (1983: 14), Lippitt and Lippitt (1994: 85), and

Lewin (1995: 179) describe professional codes of conduct for consultants.

7 Block (1999) attaches considerable value to what he calls 'authentic behaviour'. The consultant must make his or her role clear and keep it clear. This includes putting experiences into words: 'This is the most powerful thing you can do to have the leverage you are looking for and to build client commitment.' Margerison (1996: 65) gives several useful tips for making contact with the people involved and building confidence.

8 There are many good textbooks on project-based working, such as Kerzner (2003) and Turner (1998). Another book that is very suitable for fieldwork projects in practice is that by Grit (2003).

9 Many step-by-step plans for consultancy and research projects are described in the literature. These step-by-step plans differ from each other, depending on the authors' intentions (e.g. Block, 1999; Margerison, 1996; Schein, 1999; Turner, 1982; Kubr, 2002; Hale, 1998; Wickam, 2004). In general, too little attention is paid to the preliminary phase and the details of the consultancy process. This is where the TSP stands out from other publications.

There are clear parallels between the step-by-step plans for consultancy projects and the step-by-step plans for organizational research, particularly when the latter are focused on variations of the 'regulative cycle' as described by Van Strien (1997). All these step-by-step plans include a diagnostic phase, a solution phase and a change or implementation phase. See Van Aken (2004) for an example. Van Aken identifies a 'knowledge product' for each main phase: object design, implementation design and process design. There is little explicit attention paid to the preliminary phase, but there is a strong focus on effective intervention in the organization.

Chapter 2

The three main phases of the consulting process

The three main phases of the Ten-Step Plan (TSP) are the orientation phase, the research and solution phase, and the implementation phase. The TSP is shown in Figure 2.1. A copy of this Ten-Step Plan is on the bookmark. In this chapter, an outline of the three main phases is given. They will then be discussed in depth in Chapters 3–12 inclusive.

Orientation phase

Entering an unknown organization to undertake a fieldwork project is like going to stay with a family you do not yet know. They will, of course, tell you to make yourself at home. However, like all families, this family has its own way of life. As a guest, you are expected to adapt to it, but initially you do not know the house rules. So, to avoid any *faux pas*, you will behave rather carefully. After all, immediately expressing your opinions about everything and appropriating all kinds of things for yourself could be asking for problems.

People in a company also have their own manners and habits. To find out whether you, as a student, fit into that situation and can make a valuable contribution there, you act like a guest who is staying with another family for a while. You will start to explore the situation and things around you. This is what we call the orientation phase. This phase should answer the question of whether the student and the assignment principal will be able to get along and, if so, in what way. In the orientation phase as many impressions as possible will be gathered. In this phase, professional consultants

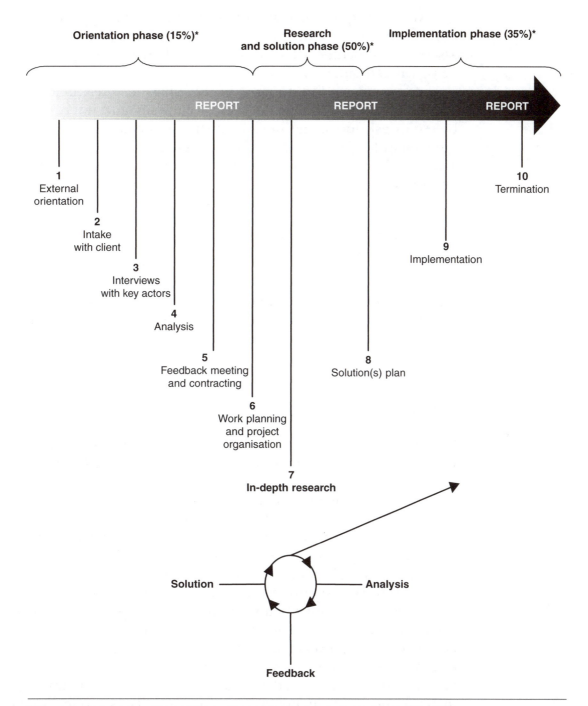

*Recommended division of time of the practical assignment period into phases of the TSP

Figure 2.1
Ten-Step Plan for practical assignments.

ask everybody questions, are interested in everything, and try to find relationships between habits, successes and problems, and assess the difficulties that might arise when the assignment is being carried out.

The best advice for students in this phase of their fieldwork project is to show similar degrees of curiosity and interest. It's better to ask too many questions than to remain silent in an 'understanding' way, for fear of being perceived as stupid or bold. The broad orientation is focused on a number of aspects of the organization:

- Culture
- The problem in its context
- Support
- The scope of the job.

We will give a short explanation of each of these aspects. The details and ways to deal with them are included in the subsequent descriptions of the various steps.

Culture

Culture encompasses all those habits that are characteristic of the way in which people in an organization collaborate. Knowledge of the culture is important if you want to play an accepted and valuable role. Organizational behaviour is only partly guided by rules, procedures and structures. Often, values and norms about how to interact with colleagues, customers and management are much more important in everyday behaviour. Culture is software but expresses itself in hard facts.[1] We have already likened starting a fieldwork assignment to staying with an unknown family. It is important to quickly understand how people interact with each other and with issues that arise. In some organizations, people quickly address each other on a first-name basis; in others, formality is the norm. In some companies, everybody is happy to help if you need assistance; in others, everything has to be requested formally via the secretary. Dress code, lunch breaks, working hours, punctuality, keeping engagements, the relationship between superiors and subordinates, openness of information, all are potential sources of misunderstanding and differences of opinion.

Every student who enters an organization to do a fieldwork project will try to adapt to a certain extent. However, the following remarks are appropriate.

Intuition

Not all habits are clear immediately and must be learned from experience. Some are apparent on the very first visit, others appear later or in special circumstances (see Case 2.1). It is important to notice them and understand them.[2] Successful consultants develop an intuition to distinguish these traits.

Case 2.1

Together with a student, one of us undertook a first visit to a company. We were welcomed by a very jovial manager, who wanted us to feel comfortable in every respect: calling each other by first names, lots of coffee, showing us the whole company and providing us with a very good lunch. On our trip home, we discussed our perceptions of the culture in the company. The student was delighted with the open, egalitarian and companionable atmosphere. He had hardly noticed how the manager had snapped at his secretary when she interrupted to ask a short question, neither had he noticed the submissive attitude of the employees towards the manager. It was clearly a manager with two faces.

A few months later, the student complained that the manager repeatedly persuaded him to disclose his research results prematurely and used these to criticize his staff.

Your own critical opinion

How far should a student go in adapting to the organization's culture? It is unwise to belie one's nature to such an extent that one no longer feels at home. In the case described above, no one would expect the student to conform to the manager's style.

But there are also less reprehensible habits to be avoided. Such habits concern, for example, the way decisions are made within organizations. Two examples are given in the following case.

Case 2.2

A student was carrying out a consulting project in a company where it appeared to be the custom to describe problems in thick reports after long and thorough investigations. The management team would discuss these reports extensively, focusing significantly on the linguistic quality of the text and the accuracy of facts and figures. Decisions on a solution and its implementation, however, were rarely made.

Another student did a project in a social welfare organization. The board of the organization said that a new strategic plan was needed. After talking with the people involved and consulting the minutes of board meetings from the previous six years, the student found that, in this period, the board had developed a strategic plan twice already. Nothing had ever been done with these plans.

In order to be successful, an alternative approach to that which these organizations had become accustomed was required. In both cases, a successful approach was used that consisted of small research and consulting steps, short presentations discussing content only, concrete decisions, and immediate implementation by work groups. By circumventing the culture of writing and discussions, the student was able to make real progress.

Considerable steadfastness is required to resist the pressure to adapt to the existing culture.[3] In the cases above, people asked repeatedly for well-documented written reports. By pointing at their earlier experiences and promising them a written report at the end of the project, the student was given the space to carry on in his own way.

The problem in its context

A second area of attention in the orientation phase concerns the problem for which the student's contribution is requested.

What is the problem?

Most often, the initial formulation of the problem is vague and ill-defined. In order to be able to formulate a *clear and broadly accepted assignment* at the end of the orientation phase, much work usually needs to be done. The best guideline for this search process is the question: What changes should have been taken place at the end of my project? If a student poses this question to some of the people involved, it forces them to be specific, and also helps very much in finding out what is or is not considered relevant. Of course, students must thus be able to form their own opinion on the contents of the assignment. A student who blindly follows the principal in his or her ideas runs the risk of not being effective. Sometimes managers have ideas about how to deal with a problem that seem to lead nowhere. A manager has often been wrestling with the issue for a long time already. The image of the problem has become deeply embedded in his or her thinking and in the organization. An original, alternative view, provided by an open-minded outsider – for instance, a student – can make new solution perspectives apparent. A critical assessment of the manager's initial wishes is therefore important.

Why has the problem not yet been solved?

The formulation of the problem is closely related to the question of why the organization has not solved the problem itself. A 'healthy' organization can solve its own problems. What is going on when outside assistance is needed? Common reasons for asking for outside assistance are:

- Lack of time to work on the problem
- Lack of knowledge
- The need for an independent opinion
- Lack of consensus among the people involved
- Other priorities.

It is of paramount importance to consider the backgrounds of an issue in the formulation of the problem and development of the approach. If management is divided on the character and urgency of the problem and/or the preferred approach to it, the student will be faced with the difficult task of finding a consensus within management. If he or she fails in that task, the project may well end with the problem still unsolved.

Where does the problem seem to be located?

The next question in the focus on the problem concerns the place in the organization where the problem is occurring, and *who the people are that are most involved*. This question is best answered during the orientation phase.

Often, the field of observation that is chosen is too narrow. Many students hold the view that the matter is settled when they have had a good discussion with a manager about the assignment. This may be true in the sense that in that case one is attuned to the person with the authority to charge someone with the assignment. However, to achieve a good level of collaboration, this discussion is not enough. For example, in a project concerning the reduction of rejects, it is advisable to also become acquainted with a number of people working in production in the plant. For an assignment involving the formulation of a marketing plan, it is essential to meet with a number of salespeople.

Furthermore, you need to size up the situation at the heart of the problem, even though it will be higher management who will take the ultimate decision on whether or not the assignment will be given.

External causes

A final area of attention concerns *external developments*. We have stated before that most bottlenecks in companies are due to external causes: changes in supply and demand, new technological developments, legislation, or labour costs. These developments have to be recognized and studied to be able to gear the solution of the problem to the cause. From experience we have found that a study of external developments is essential in all management consultancy assignments.

In Case 2.3 we give two examples where the link to external developments was not sufficiently taken into account in the research.

Case 2.3

- A company wanted to excel in providing short delivery times. The student undertaking this project did not consider the external factors and failed to notice at the start that, compared to its main competitors, the company already had the shortest delivery times and that for the coming years this would remain so. Its customers were already very satisfied with the delivery times.

It later transpired that an investment of millions of euros to shorten delivery times could not be recovered.

- A manufacturer of paints had designed 80 per cent of its production lines for filling five-litre cans. When the company started production, market demand appeared to be concentrated mainly on one-litre cans. Due to lack of capacity, the company could not follow market demand.

At the design phase of the factory, filling capacity had been approached predominantly from a logistics perspective. A consultant hired to solve this problem neglected to do research into market developments for the coming five years.

Support within the organization

As mentioned before, it is important to recognize the people who will be most involved in the assignment. Awareness of support within the organization helps to focus attention on gaining, maintaining and enhancing the involvement of those who are directly involved in the problem and any changes resulting from the project.[4]

Organizational changes can only be achieved by the people within the organization. If new working procedures are recommended, they will be the ones who will have to work according to these procedures. When such changes are developed without their involvement, the chances of their being accepted are very small. For this reason, consultants like to get in touch with people in the field, where the changes will eventually take place, during the orientation phase. Students starting fieldwork projects should also make such contacts early on in their projects. Questions that can be asked in this respect are:

- Do the people involved recognize the problem?
- Are they willing to co-operate in finding good solutions?
- Is there a positive attitude towards the student's contribution?
- Can they indicate what contributions the various people involved can make to the project?
- Do they have any concrete improvements in mind?

By communicating well with the people involved, partnerships and support for the change project are built.

The extent of the job

Like professional consultants, students have to assess the extent of the work that needs to be done. The consultant needs such an estimate to make a feasible quotation, and to provide the assignment principal and supervisors with a realistic indication of what can or cannot be done within the period agreed for the fieldwork project.[5]

Inevitably, this estimate has an arbitrary character. During each project, unforeseen circumstances occur that can affect the size of the job and the time needed. However, if one has a clear image of the intended results, many factors can be assessed beforehand. The extent of the job is determined by factors like:

- The number of people that will have to be interviewed
- The number of intermediate reports needed
- The amount of data that must be gathered
- The number of discussions of progress with supervisors and coaches
- The number of documents that have to be studied.

Many of these factors can be roughly determined in the orientation phase. For instance, when an organization's customer orientation must be improved and there is no systematic record of the customers' requirements available, a survey of customers will be needed. The time and workload of such a survey can be assessed reasonably well. By making such estimates in the orientation phase, the contracted assignment can be supplemented with a work schedule. Experience shows that well-planned projects are much more effective than the well-known hit-and-run projects, certainly when the time available is limited, as in a fieldwork project.

Since a well-executed orientation phase is crucial for a successful fieldwork project, in the Ten-Step Plan much effort is invested in this phase. No less than six of the ten steps are carried out in this initial phase – students tend to underestimate its importance. As a result, many encounter a lack of clarity and misunderstandings that could have been foreseen and prevented.

The end result of the orientation phase should be agreement between the student and assignment principal on the formulation of the problem, the formulation of the assignment and the plan of approach. This plan will guide the activities in the research and solution phase. It can only be drawn up when the student has also carried out in-depth research of the literature on the topic to be investigated. In the plan of approach, it is made clear how the goals of the fieldwork project will be met via successive or concurrent activities. It will also indicate which activities are connected and in which areas collaboration with others will be necessary. A seriously executed orientation phase will result in a clear contract in which student and organization commit themselves to the assignment.

This overall description of the orientation phase may give the impression that it requires a massive and time-consuming set of activities. It is therefore important to recognize that, for a job in a medium- to large-sized organization, a professional consultant will spend no more than a few days on this phase. For students we advise spending no more than 15 per cent of the available project time on this phase, which will be sufficient to carry out all the steps therein.

Research and solution phase

In the research and solution phase, the actual execution of the contracted assignment takes place. For this phase, less specific suggestions can be given than for the previous phase, due to the huge variation in the content of fieldwork projects. For example, the approach to be followed in developing a strategic plan differs significantly from the approach required in developing and implementing a new logistics management or information management system.

However, a number of general suggestions can be made, which will be briefly discussed here.[6] A description of how to put these into practice is given in Chapters 8–10.

For all parties involved it is important that the work schedule is in place by the end of the orientation phase. The project principal knows what to expect in terms of time to be reserved for the project and the student has committed to a work programme and time schedule. The student anticipates the activities that are on the critical path, given the agreed project planning.

Some examples of critical-path activities that occur in nearly all assignments are:

- Surveys or interviews with external parties like suppliers and customers
- Internal recording of as yet unavailable data about ongoing processes like rejects, complaints, missed orders, inventory changes and size of orders
- Management decisions that have to be taken during the project to enable progress to be made
- Reports from others that need to be elaborated on in the student's own research.

Looking back, it will often be found that overrunning the planned schedule was caused by insufficient anticipation of the fact that students in this type of work depend largely on the co-operation of other people.

When planning their approach, students like to fall back on theoretical models described in the literature. Often this is encouraged from within educational institutions, because field-work projects provide ideal opportunities to integrate theory and practice. However, an overly strong and dogmatic orientation on ready-made models from the literature can have some undesired effects. When such a theoretical model from the literature is used, one continuously has to establish whether the specific situation in the project fits the explicit assumptions behind the theoretical model.[7] Blindly applying such a model can cause the project to come to a standstill because the actual situation involved is inappropriate. In Case 2.4 we give some examples of such instances that we have encountered in practice.

Case 2.4

- A student assisted a furniture manufacturer in its stock control by introducing the well-known Camp formula. However, the degree of education of the personnel involved was so low that they did not understand the merits of the system.
- A student was assigned to help a company develop and implement an improved information system. His analysis led to a perfect system design. However, the resulting investments in hardware and software exceeded by several times the poor company results and thereby also its investment capability.

- At a metalwork company a student was supposed to design a new logistics management concept. The chosen model proved unworkable because actual quantitative data about goods flows was not available.

The development of a suitable solution for an assignment problem has an iterative character, which implies that the result of one investigation will raise new questions that necessitate further research. This character requires some flexibility and resourcefulness. If a student follows a chosen model too rigidly he or she runs the risk that they will be too busy adapting reality to the model instead of adapting the model to the specific situation in the project.

Case 2.5 shows that a search process is difficult to capture in an analytical model. Therefore, using one's common sense remains very important in the research and solution phase.

The problems illustrated in Case 2.5 can be solved but require resourcefulness and flexibility. Making a sound choice for an approach that leaves room for a solution and fits the specific circumstances can be developed by:

■ Drawing from earlier knowledge and experience, both your own and those of others. How have others dealt with comparable situations? What do you learn from your studies about this type of problem? Often, it is possible to consult the fieldwork project reports of others, or teachers who have specific knowledge. This can help get a quick overview of models and theories that can be used at the start.

■ Verifying the fit between reality and the model. What can you use from the available models and approaches in this specific situation? If done correctly, the orientation phase should have delivered sufficient data to decide on which aspects of a potential model have to be adapted, supplemented or limited to fit the situation in the project.

Case 2.5

A Danish shoe manufacturer, who was experiencing stagnation in sales, called in the help of a student. To find the root of the

contd

Case 2.5   *contd*

problem, a market survey was carried out that unexpectedly showed mainly positive developments in sales. In the sales analysis, the student noticed that the company had considerable sales to Germany.

Since Germany had been left out of the market survey, a sales analysis was done on the German customers, mainly retailers. This revealed that sales were growing, but that the number of goods returned was growing even faster. The company did not have a systematic complaints analysis process, so a number of interviews were held with German retailers. The retailers said that the reason for the returns lay in the fact that clients often noticed a faulty finish. In general, German consumers seem to adopt a more critical attitude than consumers in Denmark.

When the student informed the company about these findings, it appeared that German customers were primarily sold B-quality goods. The Sales Department, which was not responsible for German sales, wanted to keep the A-quality goods for the domestic market. In the end it was decided to also conduct a number of interviews among Danish retailers, who in general were satisfied with the quality of the shoes. They had, however, become a bit cautious in their purchasing policy due to the critical note of their German colleagues.

For students it is important that their own contribution is clearly discernible during the entire project. The project is primarily research that is carried out independently. This does not mean, however, that the student should do everything alone. It is better to include as many people as possible within the organization in the execution of the project.

Doing something *alone* has the advantage that the student can work quickly and apply his or her own knowledge. The main advantage of doing something *together* with people from the organization is that the organization learns much more – they learn to solve their own problems, and support within the organization for the project, advice and implementation is enhanced.[8]

In the chapters discussing the Ten-Step Plan we will expand upon the student's options. The main emphasis will be on involving others as much as possible.

The end result of the research and solution phase should be an effective and accepted solution for the problem described in the contracted assignment. The best test to see whether a solution is effective and acceptable is its actual implementation. We will discuss this in more detail in Chapter 10.

Implementation phase

When improvements are implemented in an organization we encounter a paradox. No one will deny that it makes sense to adopt smarter working procedures. Nevertheless, every organization has working procedures based on routines and agreements enabling people to work together efficiently. A considerable amount of management effort is spent on maintaining and improving this system of co-operation. Important changes – for example, the merger of two departments that used to work independently – will affect these organizational routines. The pressure to change is, however, steadily increasing. Many companies must continuously respond to new market demands and opportunities. Organizations should learn to deal with organizational changes, much more than with routine procedures.

Implementation of organizational changes is a difficult task. Even if a project has been carefully designed and executed, it is not certain that the resulting recommendations for change will be adopted. Case 2.6 illustrates that the urgency of a problem can change even during a fieldwork project.

Case 2.6

A manufacturer of electronic components perceived a declining turnover and assumed that this was caused by a lack of customer orientation. A student was given the task of identifying improvements via a customer survey, and to assist in their implementation. The project went well and the student identified major areas of potential improvement. When the decision had to be made to change the organization in some respects, management lost interest. Turnover was increasing again and the motivation to fundamentally improve the organization and its future competitiveness ebbed away.

Much has to be done to get everybody to work differently within a short period of time. If you want to be successful, you will have to anticipate the eventual changes as early as possible in the orientation and research and solution phases. In this respect, three success factors are important:

- Involvement
- Concreteness
- Feasibility.

Involvement

The more people within the organization that know of the project and are willing to contribute, the more they will manifest responsibility for its implementation. The feeling of being responsible for the project motivates people to work with the results.[9]

Extensive, frequent and comprehensive communication during the entire project is essential. Consultants and students who work in isolation tend to have a lesser chance of achieving real organizational changes.

Concreteness

Proposals like: 'People should work more with computers' or 'People should work more together' are of no use to an organization. These proposals are so obvious and vague that no one feels particularly concerned. Moreover, it is not made clear why many months of research were necessary. A good proposal should lead to a detailed plan of action[10] (see Case 2.7, an extract from a masters thesis).

Case 2.7

The five departments that deal with the processing and administration of orders in a company must be integrated into one department with one integrated system for order processing instead of the five subsystems that are currently used.

This integration is expected to lead to the following, clearly measurable, improvements:

- Reduction of staff by five
- Reduction of administrative errors to 1 per cent
- Shortening of order lead times to two weeks.

Feasibility

Organizational changes that look rather simple at first sight often appear to be far more complex than assumed at the time. Implementation usually raises new questions. Take, for instance, the merger of five departments in Case 2.7, where each had a sub-task in the order processing system. Observed from the outside, one might assume that the merger of two departments implies nothing more than simply bringing them together in one space. In practice, one has to answer questions like:

- Who will lead the new unit?
- Who will become redundant and what will happen to them?
- How will the tasks be divided?
- In which space will the new unit be located?
- Which working systems will be used?
- Who will become the system manager?

For the people concerned, organizational change provides chances and opportunities for improvement, but also risks and uncertainties. If these types of questions and problems are not properly recognized and addressed in the implementation phase, the whole process can fail.[11]

Conclusion

From this brief description of the success factors, the agenda for the implementation phase will have become clear: specifying the implementation activities, making decisions, assigning tasks, bringing into action new tools and resources (computers, planning boards, etc.), encouraging and training people for new tasks, discussing progress, and correcting errors.

Certain dexterity is required from students to be effective in this phase. In the TSP we will describe how to support management in this phase of the project.

Chapter notes

[1] The expression 'culture is software, but manifests itself in hard facts' originates from Hofstede (1994). Many others have pointed out the importance to a consultant or researcher of

becoming familiar with the culture of an organization. Greiner and Metzger (1983: 255) refer to the necessity of 'learning the culture'; Harvey and Brown (2005) describe the organizational culture as the entirety of accepted behaviour patterns. Culture has increasingly been viewed as dynamic and subject to change. For an overview, see Hatch (1997: 200–40).

2 Greiner and Metzger (1983) mention a number of diagnostic skills that consultants must have. In addition to qualities such as the ability to objectify, conceptualize, analyse and reason, they also mention possessing 'intense curiosity': 'Consultants must be nosy – delving behind the symptoms and superficial explanations. They are puzzle solvers who must love the challenge of a messy and ill-defined problem. The bulk of a client's problem lies beneath the tip of the iceberg.' Block (1999) shows the difference between diagnosis from a research-based approach and diagnosis from an action-based approach.

3 It is important to recognize that the consultant may start forming an opinion before becoming aware of and analysing the facts. This risk is particularly high in situations where the consultant finds him or herself on 'familiar ground'. In such cases, a consultant can give in to the temptation to make hasty judgements that are not backed by the facts and with data still to be collected.

4 Process consultants and organization developers in particular pay considerable attention to creating the necessary basis of support for their project in the organization. Schaffer (2002), for example, points out the importance of 'reducing anxiety by building confidence'. Schein (1999: 20) states as one of his five basic principles, 'It is the client who owns the problem and the solution', and also (pp. 167–8) that the nature and scale of the interventions made by a consultant should be geared, allowing the customer and consultant to reach joint diagnoses and joint decisions. Bond (in Barcus and Wilkinson, 1996: 28-1) suggests starting consultancy projects with a 'change readiness test' in which 'competence and commitment' are measured. Attention to 'exploring readiness for change' is advocated by Lippitt and Lippitt (1994).

5 Margerison (1996) stresses the importance of properly assessing the activities to be carried out. He also suggests questions

that consultants can ask when structuring their time. Grit (2003) gives many indications for drawing up a good working plan.

[6] This book does not cover the use of standardized tools such as audits. Although these tools are used in consultancy practice, it is unlikely that students will work with them (for a discussion of the possibilities, see Chambers and Rand, 1997).

[7] One of the major problems in applying theoretical models and methods is that the assumptions from which these are developed are not always immediately clear. These assumptions often include a vision of the healthy organization. Since Morgan's publication (1986) on metaphors, interest in the single or multi-perspective in organization consultancy work has increased substantially.

[8] In relation to involving members of the organization in the consultancy or fieldwork project, Overholt and Altier (1988) distinguish between a 'hard or controlling' approach on the one hand and a 'soft or flexible' approach on the other. In the first instance, the consultant has a direct influence on the thought processes of the group involved. He or she is present at and leads or directs the meetings. In the second case, the consultant provides little guidance. He or she helps to form the groups, but leaves it to the groups themselves to decide how the task will be tackled.

[9] See also Schaffer and Michaelson (1989), who consider that one of the most important success factors for a consultant is that the members of the organization feel themselves to be owners of the project: 'project ownership; guarantee to implementation'. Swieringa and Wierdsma (1992) take the same stance when they state that an organizational learning process can only be successful if those involved bear responsibility for the project themselves.

[10] Schaffer and Thomson (1992) distinguish between activity-centred and result-driven change programmes. They describe programmes of the first type as a raindance: many activities taking place simultaneously throughout the entire organization, no milestones for measuring results, activities are thought of and implemented by managers and consultants and not

by the people further down the line and on the shop floor. 'The performance improvement efforts of many companies have as much impact on operational and financial results as a ceremonial raindance has on the weather.'

[11] Greiner and Metzger (1983: 277) mention the following 'techniques' for limiting opposition to change at an early stage: commit the nay-sayers before they have expressed their opinions too emphatically; hold various sessions with members of the organization who could become involved in the changes, in which information is given and participation requested; create leeway by experimenting with change in selected segments of the organization. See also Tjosvold (1991).

Part 2

The Ten-Step Plan

Introduction to Part 2

This part describes how an effective consultancy process can be carried out. The ten steps shown in Figure 2.1 are discussed consecutively.

The contents of each step are described first – the objective, the concepts and the actions – and these are illustrated by practical examples. Several key questions are then given to summarize what should be known and achieved by the end of that step. For a fieldwork project, we recommend using these questions to check the quality of the activities within the process. We indicate in each chapter, using a randomly chosen example, how these questions can be used in practice. This will show how answering the questions will help to keep on course and ensure that no important elements are omitted. The ten checklists with questions are subsequently combined in a *Logbook* (see insert). Each chapter concludes with a list of the actions that must be carried out within that step and a number of self-study exercises.

Where timing is concerned, we have assumed that the three phases will take 15, 50 and 35 per cent respectively of the time available for the fieldwork project. However, the duration of a fieldwork period varies between courses. The problem is always whether sufficient time is available for an implementation phase. The general condition for making use of the TSP is that at the start of the project, the student, company principal and supervisors must think explicitly about what is and is not possible within the time allotted. The shorter the period available for the project, the more the student, principal and supervisors will have to think about options for limiting the scale of the assignment, so that all elements of a complete fieldwork project are adequately covered. In discussing the ten steps, the problem of correct scaling will come up regularly.

The Ten-Step Plan is a standard approach. We assume that a number of generally applicable principles can be presented for carrying out an effective fieldwork project. The practical situation naturally demands flexibility. In some cases, it may not be possible to carry out all the steps completely according to the plan. In Example 2.7, we described how a situation changed in the course of the project, which consequently changed the way the project had to be completed. It is therefore necessary to react to such new situations intelligently, in close consultation with the company and the fieldwork supervisor, depending on the circumstances. The question 'How can I get back on to the course given by the Ten-Step Plan?' should act as a guideline. If the overall structure is abandoned, it is easy for the project to become ineffective, with all the disappointments this brings with it. In Part 3, we will examine a number of exceptions to this rule.

Chapter 3

Preliminary step: Acquisition of a fieldwork project

Although strictly speaking the acquisition of the fieldwork project is not part of the TSP, its strong influence on the fieldwork project is so important that it is appropriate to discuss it here. To elucidate, we go back to one of the design criteria of the TSP, namely open contracting. This criterion concerns the formulation of the most desirable assignment via dialogue with the organization. It implies that the student must have the leeway to carry out the task.

In educational institutions, fieldwork projects and assignments can be obtained in widely diverging ways. Some can affect a student's freedom of contract more than is desirable for a successful application of the TSP model.

In practice, we have observed two main scenarios for obtaining a fieldwork project:

- After consultation with the supervisor, the student acquires a project and formulates an initial assignment completely independently
- The educational institution acquires the project, formulates the initial assignment and allocates it to the student.

Between these two extremes there are variations and combinations, depending on the specific arrangements institutions have established. A scenario is effective if it leaves the student with a reasonable level of freedom of contract. In the orientation phase, the student must have the freedom to test the validity of the draft formulation of the assignment and to make any changes or further specifications in consultation with the assignment principal.

Usually, the freedom of choice of the organization and the assignment will be restricted for good reason by the requirements of the educational institution. For instance, if one is doing a course in Facilities Management, fieldwork projects will have to be sought that are in line with this course. The scope for the fieldwork project will be somewhat broader in a Business Administration course. University education is often linked to the faculty's research activities. In such cases, fieldwork projects are occasionally sought that lie in their field of research.

In theory, these limitations in the freedom of choice do not restrict the application of the TSP model. It is crucial that there is no infringement of the student's freedom to agree on changes in the assignment based on findings in the orientation phase. After all, at the start of the project, the chosen fieldwork assignment will nearly always have an initial problem formulation that is expressed in general terms, such as:

- Design a business plan for a new activity
- Do market research into the possibilities for expansion
- Respond to new forms of competition
- Improve delivery reliability.

Experienced consultants have learnt that often the principal does not properly formulate the actual problem. They also recognize the importance of knowing the urgency of the problem and having the support to work on the problem. Moreover, such a general formulation of the assignment is insufficient to be able to correctly assess what the final outcome of the job will be and what budget will be required. These are reasons for not accepting an assignment straight away, but first checking and specifying the formulation of the problem by means of orientational interviews.

For a fieldwork project, the orientation phase of the TSP always has the same objective. It is instructive for students and necessary for a successful fieldwork project that they independently check the formulation of the problem. However, fieldwork supervisors and others involved in the acquisition of fieldwork projects sometimes see such professional freedom as improper frankness, showing a lack of trust in their choice and instructions. This is even more pronounced if the person who acquired the fieldwork project has not limited himself or herself to the agreed parameters of the problem, but has already questioned its depth at the intake meeting. For those undertaking fieldwork projects and for fieldwork supervisors, it is important to realize that, by their actions, they unintentionally contribute to a greater risk of failure and deny students an important learning opportunity.

Undoubtedly, every educational institution will have good reasons for their present method of acquiring fieldwork projects. Sometimes the numbers are so high that a certain mass approach to the acquisition process is necessary. In this case, they put up with the almost inevitable superficiality of the selection work. They then draw on their regular network of usually large organizations that guarantee, for instance, ten fieldwork projects that will subsequently be made more specific. They will worry later about the urgency of the assignments that still need to be specified, and about their orientation to change.

This type of acquisition is understandable, but usually it can be done in a better way. That is why we now describe a preferable acquisition scenario. This description is based on our own experience as supervisors of fieldwork projects and our observations in other institutions. The approach is an important time saver for the institution and is beneficial to the quality of the learning process and the applicability of the TSP.

The basic assumption is that in principle students acquire their own fieldwork projects. To support them in this process, educational institutions provide a list of requirements for fieldwork projects. Such a list may require that projects should:

- be suitable for the course (to be specified further) and the student
- be located in a certain region, with a view to the practicality of supervision
- be feasible within the allocated time with respect to size and complexity
- be directed at an organizational change that is to be implemented during the fieldwork project
- offer the possibility of working according to the TSP
- be directed at an urgent problem
- be approved by the project supervisor.

To obtain such a fieldwork project, students should select 10–25 organizations where they expect that such problems exist. If the student would like to work on customer orientation, it may be worthwhile trying to get a project in a privatized or not-for-profit organization (post office, railway companies, hospitals) and in organizations that have internal services.

For assignments aimed at logistic improvements, students should concentrate on companies with large flows of goods that are being forced into more efficient production and distribution methods by fierce competition – for instance, supermarkets and industrial enterprises. This will also make it necessary for them to decrease their logistics costs.

The student will discuss his or her selection with the fieldwork supervisor and draw up a letter of solicitation. After having contacted the organization by telephone to ask for the name of the person in charge of allocating fieldwork projects, a personalized letter is sent. In the letter, the student states that within one to two weeks he or she will call to hear whether there is the possibility of doing a fieldwork project.

On average, about 10 per cent of these letters receive a positive response. Having a choice between two or three potential projects will increase the chance that at least one will be suitable (which is why we suggest sending 25 letters).

An example of such a letter sent by a Dutch student is shown below.

Example 3.1

To Candle Manufacturer
Intimate Lighting
Attn. Mr Peter Thompson

Groningen, 5 September 2005

Dear Mr Thompson,
I am sending this letter as I am looking for a post to carry out my fieldwork project.

I am currently doing a course in Business Administration at the Hanze College in Groningen. In a few months, I will enter the fourth year of the course. An important part of that year, over a period of five months, will be spent on a fieldwork project.

In consultation with my fieldwork supervisor, Mrs M. de Vreeze, B.Eng., I have decided to try to find a fieldwork project in which I can work on a customer orientation problem. This decision is influenced greatly by the interest with which I have followed the lectures on marketing in which customer orientation was discussed. The fact that the Dutch business community is occupying itself with this type of quality improvement appeals to me very much.

Quite by coincidence I heard that your sector is also considering taking steps to measure customer satisfaction. Evidently, your customers increasingly demand such actions as well.

This gave me the idea to enquire whether your company might also have plans to work on customer satisfaction. If that were indeed the case, would it be possible for me to assist you in that activity in a fieldwork project?

I have enclosed my CV. I would be delighted to hear that it proves I am the right person for a possible fieldwork project in your company.

To reiterate, the duration of this project will be five months, starting January 2006. The project has to offer the opportunity to work on research that is oriented toward concrete organizational change. In my opinion, measuring and improving customer satisfaction will certainly meet that requirement.

I would like to hear whether you might be interested in engaging me in a fieldwork project on the subject mentioned above. I shall contact you in the week of 13 September next (week 37) by telephone to learn your reaction.

Yours sincerely,

Frits Jongstra

Enc. CV

The student will visit each of the organizations that responded positively to discuss the general content and urgency of the assignment, and request some documentation on the organization. The student informs the organization that there are more prospective projects and that he or she will visit other organizations as well, after which a choice will be made in consultation with the project supervisor. The student will agree on a deadline to inform the organization about this final choice.

The final decision will be made together with the supervisor, partly on the basis of the list of criteria. One of the difficulties in this process is in assessing the feasibility of the assignment in the time that is reserved for the fieldwork project. In particular, if, in accordance with the TSP, one wants to reach the implementation phase, the assignment should not be too extensive. It still remains difficult to assess, but there are some indicators of the complexity of the assignment to consider, such as:

- The number of employees in the business unit concerned
- The number of people directly involved in the field of research
- Available information and the amount and degree of complexity of data that still needs to be gathered
- Spread to other sub-organizations
- Spread to the external environment
- Dependence on others in the execution of the assignment
- The student's expertise and knowledge with respect to the field of research
- The concreteness and visibility of the work processes involved
- Available possibilities for performance measurement

- Distance of communication between the student and the people who have to decide on his or her proposals
- Accuracy and decisiveness in the organization that is offering the assignment.

In most cases, the student will already prefer a specific project. Unless there are good reasons to do otherwise, supervisors should go with that preference. When students inform an organization of their decision to choose another fieldwork assignment, they should try to keep the rejected assignment available for another student within the educational institution. If the companies involved are willing to be introduced to the fieldwork project co-ordinator or the bureau acquiring fieldwork projects, a reserve of qualifying assignments can be created for students who have not succeeded in acquiring their own fieldwork project. Often, organizations do not object to getting a second chance of finding a student to work for them.

The benefits of this approach are obvious. Students learn to apply for a position, they keep the maximum latitude for negotiations with respect to the subsequent exploration and specification of the assignment, and the person involved in the acquisition of fieldwork projects is relieved of an important burden. Moreover, it certainly provides more variation in the types of companies offering fieldwork assignments and a larger and more extensive network for the educational institution.

Finally, it is important to bear in mind that some possible assignments are not appropriate for students in a fieldwork project. It is obvious that students and supervisors need to ask themselves whether they can obtain and provide the necessary knowledge and skills required for the assignment. Developing and implementing a strategic plan for a company may seem a challenging task for an MBA student. However, besides knowledge about making external and internal analyses, such an assignment often also requires professional skills in developing consensus between people who have strong personal opinions. An MBA student can no doubt carry out the analyses and deliver a report that can be input for a management team discussion about strategic options, but most likely the consensus and decision-making part is unachievable. This does not mean that in this particular case a student cannot achieve an academically and practically useful result. If the student is allowed to interview the members of the management team individually, to establish a short list of the team members' different expectations, wants and wishes, and from there develop strategic options, gather data, and analyse and interpret the data, this will be a satisfactory assignment. It often helps to have an open talk about expectations and possibilities.

Less obvious and more difficult to identify, in reality, is that sometimes managers or management teams have hidden agendas behind assignments that look feasible at first sight. If a student is invited to carry out an efficiency study in one of the organizational units this assignment may be a neutral starting point for an internal discussion about improving processes and procedures. However, an efficiency study may also be meant as a step to provide further arguments for an already-made decision to slim down the organization. In such cases of a strategic or political nature, students will soon discover that employees are not willing to co-operate and that people will very much mistrust what they are doing.

We will return to this problem later in elaborating the steps of the TSP.

List of action points

The activities described in this chapter are summarized as follows:

1. Write a letter of application and discuss it with the project supervisor
2. Select 10–25 suitable companies
3. Send letters and do a follow-up by telephone
4. Visit the companies that showed interest
5. Make the final choice in consultation with the supervisor
6. Introduce the companies whose projects were rejected to the bureau/person acquiring fieldwork projects.

Chapter 4

Step 1: External orientation

The external orientation involves a limited pre-study of the organization where the fieldwork project will be carried out and the sector in which the organization is active. This study takes place *after* the organization in which the fieldwork assignment will be carried out has been identified, but *before* the student has his or her first official conversation (intake meeting) with the assignment principal. The objective of the external orientation is to obtain the information and insights needed for a successful intake meeting.

When obtaining consulting assignments, professional consultants often find themselves in a competitive situation. By gathering information on the organization and its sector in advance, they are able to prepare themselves for the first meeting. Thus, they can ascertain whether there is a connection between the problem outlined by the company and developments within the line of business, and if so, what the exact nature of this connection is.

In most cases, such a connection does indeed exist, and having a clear understanding of its nature is essential. If a not-for-profit organization is seeking assistance in commercializing an internal service, a connection with external developments will not be immediately apparent. Gaining insight into the government's decreasing readiness to subsidize organizations will show things in a different light. Being able to bring up this connection at the intake meeting will help to obtain better insight into the budgetary needs of the organization and the urgency of its intended action. This insight also helps to consider alternative measures at the appropriate time in the consultation process. After all, the objective of the assignment is no longer to commercialize the service, but to solve the organization's budgetary needs, which probably can be done better and more quickly in a different way.

For students the situation is often slightly different. In most cases, an acquisition meeting has taken place before the official intake meeting, either with the student or with a representative of the educational institution. Inevitably, in such a case there will already have been a general formulation of the assignment. However, it is still advisable to create some leeway for an external orientation. In practice, this can be done by making a clear distinction between the acquisition meeting and the formal intake meeting in the contacts with the organization. Whoever is acquiring the project – the educational institution's representative or the student – will inform the organization of the fact that after a possible initial agreement on the fieldwork project, an intake meeting with the student and his or her supervisor will still have to follow about the possible approach and actions needed to solve the problem. The intake meeting will entail a much more in-depth discussion of both parties' objectives and wants.

The external orientation can be assessed between the two meetings, and will, for that matter, have the same objectives as the work of a professional consultant. Even though the formal acquisition has taken place, many decisions on the contents of the assignment, the reason for the assignment, and what will lie within or outside the student's remit to carry out the assignment still have to be made before the project can actually commence. A student who has prepared well for the intake meeting, and consequently is a good discussion partner for the assignment principal, can thus lay a good foundation for an effective consulting project.

In the acquisition meeting, some students ask for information about the company and its sector. Of course, that is a sensible thing to do, but it does not suffice. There is a great chance that they will obtain slightly biased information, since they will only get what the company *itself* knows and thinks about itself and its line of business. External sources can provide important additional information. Case 4.1 gives an example of such a surprising outcome.

Case 4.1

A consultant visited a British company manufacturing wooden transportable living units to discuss assisting it in its

contd

Case 4.1 *contd*

effort to design a strategic plan to counteract a decrease in turnover. At the first meeting, the consultant asked, among other things, about the number of competitors the company had. The managing director estimated this number at five to ten. In his external orientation, the consultant had also carried out research on the competition by looking at the advertisements in trade journals to see which companies were offering transportable living units. He had counted at least 50, and had also observed that almost every one of them offered synthetic units. So, the number of competitors was considerably larger than the managing director thought and market demand had probably shifted from wooden to synthetic units.

The external orientation can be carried out on the basis of a number of questions, which are given in the checklist (see Table 4.1). The answers in the checklist have been derived from an actual case where a housing corporation requested assistance in designing and implementing a strategic plan.

The external orientation revealed that, in general, housing corporations are facing lack of occupancy and the effects of decreasing housing benefits. In addition, supervision from the Ministry of Housing has increased. In the region where this corporation was established, there are well over 700 housing corporations with a total number of houses of about 2.3 million units. This specific housing corporation was one of the smaller corporations. In the larger cities, housing corporations often have over 20 000 units. For several years, the housing corporation in question had a lack of occupancy of about 15 per cent, resulting in a structural loss in operating income. A merger with one or several smaller corporations operating in the same region could provide considerable advantages with respect to capacity. However, there is no management consensus on this subject, which has resulted in a crisis in management decision-making. As the council wants to see progress, the corporation decided to seek outside assistance in their strategic planning.

Obviously, in this type of research many more questions can be posed than those mentioned in the checklist. This checklist indicates which subjects must at least be considered in all cases,

Table 4.1

Example of a completed logbook page for Step 1

Checklist – Step 1: External orientation	
Questions	**Answers**
1 To what sector does the organization belong?	• Social sector housing
2 What are the most important sector developments?	• Lack of occupancy – decreasing subsidies – increasing government supervision from the Ministry of Housing
3 What is the organization's position in the sector?	• Size: 3500 houses (small) • Employees: 35 • Largest of four regional housing corporations
4 What are the recent developments within the organization?	• Management crisis • Rumours of a merger • Loss-making position

5 What are the influences of sector developments and recent organizational developments on the expected assignment?	• Strategic plan needed for:
	  – Improvement of results
	  – More market-directed thinking
	  – Ending the management crisis

6 Remarks	
Source: local press via the Internet.	

as a basic agenda for the external orientation in the fieldwork project.

By completing the checklist, some interesting data was found for the housing corporation. Naturally, a consultant who is aware of this data can conduct a better intake meeting than one who has not done any form of orientation and still has to ask all kinds of questions. The latter runs the risk that he or she will not be informed immediately about a number of things.

Where is such information to be found? What are the best available sources for such external research that must be carried out independently?

An important first step in the search process is to determine to which industrial or trading section the company belongs. A considerable amount of statistical industrial data has been collected and recorded by branches of industry. The correct determination of the branch of industry the company is in will open up a world of relevant statistics. Governments have statistical services and the European Commission has Eurostat. All these offices provide Internet services that can easily be consulted once it is known to which branch the company involved belongs. This does not mean, of course, that merely copying some statistics will suffice for a thorough external orientation. Data must be analysed and interpreted to find any trends that may clarify the formulation of the problem of the fieldwork assignment. The key question in this exercise is 'What is the connection between the developments in the line of business and the problem formulation?' (question 1.5 in the logbook). A business-specific problem – for example, a question of succession – often requires different interventions than a problem that involves the entire sector.

The Internet offers unprecedented possibilities. However, a warning is called for here. If one looks only at the website of the company one is gathering information about, one must realize that this information is that which the company has intentionally published about itself. A full external orientation must be more comprehensive.

After having answered the question about the correct branch of the industry, the subject of what sources of information are available comes up. We mention here some general sources, but it should be stressed that this is not an exhaustive account. For each individual case, additional specific sources of information can often be found as well.[1]

In addition to the statistical offices, a few other sources can be consulted to build a picture of the company within its environment:

- *Banks*. Banks closely follow the trends and developments in trade and industry. A number of larger banks periodically publish material on the trends in various sectors of trade and industry. These publications are usually available on request.
- *Newspapers and trade press*. Daily and weekly papers often publish articles on companies and/or lines of business with publicity value. Examples are:
  - multinationals and large concerns
  - enterprises that are quoted on the stock exchange
  - utility companies
  - successful and failing companies
  - companies with much-talked-about CEOs.

The trade press is particularly useful as a means of gaining a more focused insight into a particular line of business. It contains sector-specific articles and often other companies in the sector advertise in their columns. Browsing through one or two volumes can often be very informative. In some cases, it can be difficult to identify the trade journal of a specific sector. There are libraries that keep abreast of a large number of trade journals and publish so-called sector outlines.

■ *Sector associations*. Many sectors and lines of business have their own associations with a relatively high number of participants. The aim of these associations is to act as interest groups for their members. They offer a meeting point for consultation on and discussion of various subjects. They often collect and distribute statistical information. Official positions are taken on government policy and other important developments.

■ *Experts in the field*. Sometimes there are people or organizations that are knowledgeable about a particular sector through their contacts or experience. These can be specialist consultants, professors or teachers. These people or organizations are sometimes difficult to trace. A good way to find them is to make enquiries in various places. The trade journals may also put you on the right track to find this type of expert.

These sources of information for external orientation will help to gain useful insights into a company and its sector.

Sometimes there is not enough time for an extensive study of the available sources and it is necessary to carry out a quick orientation about a company. Case 4.2 shows what can be done in such a case.

Case 4.2

A student received a positive reply to her letter. She was invited by an electricity company to visit them in the near future to discuss a possible fieldwork project assignment. There was not enough time to obtain in-depth documentation. What should she do? In order to have some level of preparation for the meeting, she had the idea of phoning some acquaintances that lived in that particular area and asking them whether they knew anything about their regional electricity company. From the various pieces of information gleaned, mainly consisting of what had appeared in local newspapers, a picture of the company emerged. In the recent past, it had tried several times to merge with other electricity companies. Each time these attempts had failed. During the intake meeting it appeared that the company was looking for somebody who could design and help implement an improved system for measuring client satisfaction, an issue related to the failure of the attempted mergers, because their potential merger partners had wanted to see objective data about client satisfaction.

List of action points

To conclude Step 1, we summarize the actions that need to be carried out in the external orientation phase:

1 Describe the problem that most probably has to be addressed in the project
2 Decide what external information may be needed, given the assumed content of the project
3 Select the sources where the necessary information can be found
4 Gather the information
5 Summarize the data found in a coherent report
6 Complete the relevant page of the logbook.

Chapter notes

[1] See also Kubr (2002: 143) and, for similar advice, Biech (1999: 158–9). Biech gives the following two tasks to be addressed in advance:

1 Obtain the best public information available about the organization and the industry
2 Learn the general industry jargon.

Exercises for Step 1

4.1 Metalware Ltd

Metalware Ltd is a medium-sized manufacturer of hinges and locks. It has about 300 employees, the majority of which are well trained in the field of machine work.

The annual turnover is in the region of €35 million and is predominantly generated by superior quality hinges and locks for commercial and industrial building and house-building. The majority of the goods sold are produced by the company itself. The rest are bought and sold on to its customers without any processing. This section of the product range amounts to about €7.5 million of the total turnover.

Sales are largely made to builders' merchants, who sell the goods to contractors. A small but fast-growing part of the turnover is obtained from hardware shops who deliver directly to the end users – mainly house owners. In this section of trade, the range of hinges and locks for protection against burglary are particularly in demand.

1 Carry out an external orientation on Metalware Ltd. Start from the assumption that the intended fieldwork assignment will be focused on the question of whether the company is still competitive with its cost price for self-produced hinges and locks or whether there is good reason to switch further from in-house production to buying and reselling.

2 Describe the data you looked for but could not find.

4.2 Electricon

Electricon is an electricity company in the Netherlands. You are negotiating with this company about a possible fieldwork assignment in view of the increasing competition in the energy sector.

The question is how Electricon's kWh price compares to the prices charged by domestic competitors.

1 Carry out an external orientation in preparation for the intake meeting and write a well-documented report on the results.

2   Will this assignment be extensive enough to occupy the time available for your fieldwork project?
3   What is known about electricity exports and imports?
4   What are the prospects for nuclear energy production in Europe?

Chapter 5

Step 2: The intake meeting

The first meeting with a potential principal is called the intake meeting. In consultancy, this is a meeting in which client and consultant become acquainted, unless the consultant has worked for the client before on another assignment. In that case, after getting reacquainted, they will soon move on to the meeting's second topic of conversation: the assignment.

Students doing a fieldwork project have often already attended an acquisition meeting before the intake meeting. Since acquisition must be carried out to find a fieldwork project, such an assignment is usually obtained by an *offer* from the educational institution or by the actions of students themselves; a consultant is usually *invited* by the principal.

This difference in the acquisition procedure of a fieldwork assignment requires some attention. The *objective* of the intake meeting is to find out whether there is a basis for successful implementation of the assignment. The final decision on the nature of and approach to the project will only be taken in Step 5, upon completion of a thorough orientation. One should avoid making the assignment too restrained via agreements made during the acquisition and intake meetings.[1] Some leeway is needed to be able to determine, on the basis of the orientation, what results the project should aim to achieve, and in what way and under what conditions these results can be achieved. In this way, wants and possibilities can be better geared to each other and disappointments can be prevented. To obtain this leeway, it is very important to continuously be aware of the final objective of the discussion:

- ■ Final objective of the acquisition meeting – to determine that there is a fieldwork project available, enabling one to work on a topic that is generally agreed upon.
- ■ Final objective of the intake meeting – to come to an agreement that student X will start on a given date with an internal orientation to further define the intended topic of the project and to convert it into a definite assignment formulation and a plan of action.

Describing the objective of the intake meeting in this way implies that it is the student who has to hold the intake meeting. To ensure that the draft assignment meets the requirements of the educational institution, it is preferred that the fieldwork supervisor is present during this meeting.

Taking responsibility for the formulation of the assignment is a very important learning experience for students. Students will clearly look at the assignment differently and have greater motivation if their supervisor and assignment principal consult them about these arrangements. The importance of the intake meeting will be apparent from the information the student will be able to write down in the logbook's checklist afterwards. In the checklist for this step (Table 5.1), the results are given from the intake meeting at the paint factory mentioned in Case 2.4, which in practice was unable to achieve the production capacity that was intended in the factory design. The answers are derived from the report the student made about the intake meeting he and his fieldwork supervisor had with the prospective principal.

Since a fieldwork student must try to obtain a large amount of information in a relatively short time (about 1.5 hours), a good agenda is absolutely indispensable. With their experience, professional consultants may be able to draw up an agenda even during the meeting in consultation with the other people present. Students should spend time in advance on this and have a draft agenda ready for distribution at the meeting. Obviously, it must be flexible enough to enable the discussion partner to add other items.

It is advisable to discuss your draft agenda beforehand with your fieldwork supervisor, who should also be present at the intake meeting. Thus, his or her possible suggestions for improvement can be incorporated in advance, which will avoid any discussion

Table 5.1
Example of a completed logbook page for Step 2

Checklist – Step 2: Intake meeting with the client	
Questions	**Answers**
1 What is the problem according to the assignment principal?	• The new factory does not work at intended capacity
2 What is the urgency of solving the problem?	• High; market growth creates delivery problems, resulting in decrease in market share
3 What has caused the problem?	• Presumably a misfit between the planned container dimensions in the factory design and those demanded by the market
4 What has been done internally to solve it?	• Work group with members from Engineering and Marketing; deadlocked
5 Who are the most involved parties?	• Head of Engineering, production manager, head of Marketing, head of the Works Office, head of Sales
6 Who will be the assignment principal or company coach?	• Production manager
7 What will be the desired end result of this fieldwork project according to the assignment principal?	• A feasible plan for adaptation of the production lines and the start of the plan's implementation
8 How will the student be introduced?	• Introduction in a meeting of the management team • Announcement in staff magazine, *Thinner*

9 What are the follow-up arrangements on:
  a Orientational interviews
  b Date of feedback meeting
	• The parties directly involved (see item 5)
	• Arrangement for start of interviews is being made

10 Remarks	

at the intake meeting. You can also use this opportunity to discuss the role of the fieldwork supervisor during the meeting. Although the student is supposed to hold the conversation, given his or her own responsibility for the assignment, this will not always be possible without making arrangements in advance. A managing director will automatically address the most senior visitor first. If the fieldwork supervisor goes along with this, it will be difficult for the student to assume the role of main discussion partner and he or she will lose the initiative. For this reason, the fieldwork supervisor is advised to adopt a reserved attitude, particularly at the outset of the meeting. As fieldwork supervisors we choose to mention explicitly at the beginning of the meeting that we are only present in an accompanying role and that the consultation should primarily be between the student and the company representative.

An example of an agenda for the intake meeting is given below.

Example 5.1: Draft agenda intake meeting on ... from 09.00 to 10.30 hrs

1   Introduction
2   Objective
3   Exchange of information on the organization and the assignment
4   Exchange of information on the course and the objective of the fieldwork project
5   Appointment of the company coaches and the manner of supervision
6   Exchange of information on the execution of the project in accordance with the TSP
7   Follow-up arrangements on:
    •   starting date
    •   orientational interviews and respondents
    •   contents and date of feedback session (Step 5)
    •   manner of student's introduction in the company
    •   student's pay.
8   Site visit.

This agenda shows that many matters require attention. We will now discuss the most important items on this agenda.

During the *introduction*, it is important to gain insight into the position(s) of the discussion partner(s). Usually, decisions on hiring a consultant or fieldwork student are made by a limited number of people at the top of the organization. If the discussion partner is part of this group, it is possible to come to decisions during the meeting. Otherwise, decisions can only be made after internal consultation with the decision-maker. For this reason, an intake meeting with one of the decision-makers is preferred.[2]

For professional consultants, direct contact with top management is also important for various other reasons. Assignments often involve large consultancy fees, which are decided at the 'very top'. However, for a consultant it is just as important to be in direct contact with the top manager when carrying out the consulting work. Close contact increases the chance that the advice will indeed be implemented. Therefore, the consultant prefers to enter via top management and this plays a role from the very first meeting.

The top manager also has an interest in selecting the consultants personally and getting to know them well. He often places delicate problems in the hands of the consultant, making the success of his own company partly dependent on this consultant. For this reason, the manager is looking for someone trustworthy. The first meeting – which is often also used as a selection tool – plays an important role in creating a relationship based on trust. For all these reasons, the professional consultant will usually meet with people from top management. In Case 5.1, an example is given of how this can sometimes go wrong in practice.

In fieldwork assignments, things are usually different. In general, fieldwork assignments are considered to be less important to the company, which is illustrated by the more subordinate position of the discussion partner at the meeting. However, for a successful implementation of the assignment, good contact with the decision-makers is also important for students. It is therefore advisable to bring up the desirability of the presence of such a contact at the intake meeting. If the discussion partner is not in a top management position, it will certainly be possible to try to arrange an interview at this level in subsequent meetings.

Case 5.1

A consultant was invited to a university training institution for a consulting assignment. The intake meeting took place with the chairperson of the University Works Council (UWC), who in daily life worked in the technical services department. The chairperson explained that the problem involved the details of a reduction in staff numbers. Dissent had arisen between the UWC and the board on the technical services department's role in the cutbacks. Since the UWC had the right to have an independent investigation carried out, the chairperson had arranged this meeting.

The meeting had barely started when a rather heated man entered the room. He appeared to be the secretary of the board, who started a discussion then and there with the UWC chairperson about whether the chairperson had the authority

contd

Case 5.1   *contd*

to commission a research assignment. The consultant tried to mediate in this dispute, but to no avail. There was then nothing left for the consultant to do but express his willingness to carry out the assignment, after they had reached agreement about it internally.

An awkward situation that often occurs during intake meetings is that the consultant or student, in their zeal to sell themselves well, talks nineteen to the dozen. This sales argument of course only holds in part. Experience shows, however, that one serves one's own interests better by listening attentively and asking the right questions than by presenting oneself too emphatically at this stage. In particular, one should give the host the opportunity to talk at length about item 3 on the agenda − *the organization and the fieldwork assignment*.[3] This will give the consultant or student a more detailed picture of what lies ahead.

It is important that the consultant or student makes extensive notes. Even someone with a very good memory will forget details and will eventually fall back on a limited number of main issues. There are, of course, also items that have already been put in writing and of which copies can be requested, such as:

- Organization charts
- Company brochures
- Annual reports
- Internal notes on the organizational problem to be discussed
- The staff magazine
- Minutes of relevant meetings on the problem
- Market research and consulting reports.

It is advisable to take this type of documentation with you or, if that is not possible, to ask for copies to be sent later.

Of the documentation mentioned above, the organization chart is particularly important because it gives the names of the managers and the number of employees they have in their charge. It provides insight into the way the company activities have been organized, which part of the organization is faced with the problem and who are the most important managers there. It also shows the position within the organization of your discussion partner.

In practice, a problem – particularly in smaller companies – is often that no organization chart is available. In smaller companies, people know each other, making it unnecessary to chart the entire organization. A good solution then is to ask your discussion partner to draw up such a chart during the meeting.

It goes without saying that the formulation of both the problem and the assignment must also be discussed extensively. At the meeting, the student should at least reach the point where he or she understands why the company is faced with the problem and why solving it is so important. This means that the student should continue asking questions until this is clear. The checklist in Table 5.1 provides some useful assistance here. If we take a closer look at this checklist, we will notice that it does not contain any obvious questions, such as:

- How large is the company?
- What products does it make?
- What does the organization look like?
- How has the production process been organized exactly?
- Do you contract out much of the work?
- What is the target group of your company?
- How large is your market share?
- How have sales and distribution been organized?
- How high is customer satisfaction?

We call questions of this type *organizational* questions, as opposed to the more *change-directed* questions in the checklist in Table 4.1. Organizational questions are aimed particularly at the description and operation of the company and the possibilities for change. One needs to have some insight into this at the intake meeting to be able to assess the problem, but the orientational interviews will contribute largely to this insight. Change-directed questions are more focused on the change aspect of the consulting assignment. Like a fieldwork assignment, a consulting assignment has the objective of bringing about organizational change in the indicated problem area. Early insight into the possibility for change determines – sometimes even more than the organizational aspects – whether the consultant/student will take on the assignment.

Experience shows that by their very nature the organizational aspects dominate any discussion on the potential for change during an intake meeting. This can be explained by the primary interests of the discussion partners. A managing director likes to talk about pride in the company and how that has been achieved.

The student is eager to learn and wants to know everything on the subject. Moreover, a student is looking in particular for a 'nice' fieldwork company and whether this is so will be apparent from the presentation of the company. A result of this one-sidedness, which constantly looms, may be that subsequently the student still does not have any idea about the chances and risks involved in getting organizational change implemented in that company. To reduce the risk of poor change-directed insight, the checklist in Table 5.1 mainly includes change-directed questions. The organizational questions will follow as a matter of course.

Another factor the student must pay attention to is the possibility that his or her research coincides with that of other students and/or consultancies. Recently, one of us had to deal with a fieldwork project that coincided with two consulting assignments that had been started earlier in the fields of Business Process Redesign – a customer-oriented organizational redesign – and ERP, an information system for production control. The student who was to start a project on parts stock control had heard about those activities but had not tried to co-ordinate them in the project. Subsequently it appeared that some activities in his project overlapped those of the consultancies.

Several change processes taking place concurrently with no co-ordination between them can be detrimental to organizations. For individuals or departments this can result in conflicting change actions. A consequence may be that none of the organizational changes will be fully developed. Our experience is that managers, who after all employ all these consultants at the same time, are not always fully aware of this need for co-ordination. It is therefore advisable that students enquire about other consulting projects that may overlap with their fieldwork project. If any overlap is found, it is advisable to try to arrange meetings with the other people involved so that all the activities taking place are complementary.

The agenda also contains items 4 and 6, which involve the exchange of *information* about the place of the *fieldwork assignment* in the course of study and the approach in accordance with the *TSP*. This is certainly important because it raises the question of the company's responsibility for the success of the fieldwork project. It is better to agree on any limitations or objections on the part of the company as early as at the intake meeting, instead of being unpleasantly confronted with them at some later stage in the project. During the intake meeting both parties still have the opportunity to part company amicably if the wants and possibilities do not fit. If a fieldwork assignment is offered that does not leave enough leeway for a successful result and a good learning experience, it is better to stop and look for another project. Continuing in such a situation will almost certainly lead to significant problems later on in the project. Case 5.2 shows how a fieldwork project can go wrong.

Case 5.2

A student from the USA had made arrangements to undertake a graduation project with a company in Singapore. A number of faxes had been exchanged about the problem and the assignment. During the intake meeting in Singapore it appeared that the ideas of the student and the assignment principal about the contents and form of the project differed greatly. The student wanted to carry out independent research. The assignment principal disagreed – the student would not be able to carry out interviews and various pieces of necessary information were unavailable. The company had thought that the student just wanted to gain practical work experience abroad for a few months. After consultation by fax with his graduation supervisor, the student decided to start working after all and hope for the best. When he had finished his time with the company and returned to the USA to write his report, it appeared that the material he had gathered was lacking in various essential areas. To the frustration of everyone involved, the final report was rejected and the student had to start a new graduation project.

Item 5 of the agenda brings up the position of the *company coach*. A good company coach is vital for the quality of the fieldwork project. The tasks of the company coach are:

- Acting as daily guide to the student
- Taking care of the student's introduction
- Making arrangements and opening doors for the student
- Allocating budgets – for instance, for market research or visits to industrial exhibitions
- Giving advice and monitoring progress
- Evaluating the student and his or her work
- Acting as a link to top management.

Sometimes the functions of the assignment principal and the company coach are carried out by the same person. This often happens when projects are carried out in smaller companies. This is a welcome bonus for the student.

Obviously, a student will work very independently, making intensive supervision unnecessary, but at decisive moments the coach is essential. For this reason, it is advisable to discuss the requirements the company coach must meet during the intake meeting.[4] With respect to the coach's tasks mentioned above, the requirements can be formulated as indicated below. The company coach must have or be:

- a top or senior management position within the company
- at least a few years' work experience within the company
- an educational level at least equalling that of the student
- broad knowledge of and access to all company divisions
- an interested party in the project
- available during the period of the project
- generally accepted within the company.

The student will not always be in a position to get all his or her wants, which does not mean, however, that they cannot be brought up for discussion. Since there will be more opportunity to make arrangements at the beginning of the assignment than halfway through the project, when problems due to weak liaison become apparent, the intake meeting is the best time to discuss these subjects.

If it appears that the discussion partner will also be the intended company coach and – by the available criteria – seems to be unsuitable for that position, the student will be placed in a difficult position. This subject would therefore need attention during the acquisition meeting, to avoid an embarrassing situation occurring during the intake meeting. However, if a student encounters this problem, the most elegant way out may be to start with this coach for the time being and to arrange that the issue of suitability be looked at again at a later date. After all, once the next step in the consultation process – the orientational interviews – is completed, the student will know more people within the company, which will make a possible change in coach easier to discuss.

Finally, we would like to draw attention to the *follow-up arrangements* item on the agenda. In doing so, we inevitably anticipate a number of steps that still have to follow in the overall consultation process. The subsequent step in the TSP – Step 3 – concerns the orientational interviews aiming to better acquaint the student with the organization and the problem concerned. Usually, there are five to ten people that bear responsibility in the research area in question. The selection, which can best be done during the intake meeting, based on the organization chart, should be made with the necessary care. The objective of the orientational interviews is to gather enough information to be able to draw up a fieldwork project contract that will be satisfactory to all parties. Case 5.3 points out the risk of an ineffective contract being made, if the student has not spoken to the right people.

Case 5.3

A sales manager called in a student for an assignment to improve the organization's customer orientation. Neither initially realized that this assignment not only touched on the area of responsibility of the sales manager, but also on that of the entire management team. When finally attention was drawn to this fact during a meeting with the fieldwork supervisor, it was decided to involve the entire management team in the assignment by means of orientational interviews.

To select the right people to interview, it is best to first ask the company's representative at the intake meeting for a list of suggestions. This proposal can then be discussed on the basis of the organizational chart and changed if necessary. The key factor in this process remains the extent to which the potential interviewees are involved in the area of research. This involvement can vary considerably. The person in question may be:

- co-responsible for the field of research – for instance, as manager
- the one who is faced with the problem – for instance, a warehouse foreman with respect to stock management that is out of control
- the victim – for instance, in the case of a possibly painful but necessary change in position
- entitled to give advice with respect to the field of research – for instance, the staff manager with respect

to a compensation problem or (as is often the case) the entitlement of the works council to give advice on an organizational audit.

The last of these in particular – the entitlement of the works council to give advice – is often overlooked. An orientational interview with the chairperson of the works council can clarify and support matters and prevent opposition at the later stages of the consulting project.

The report on the interview findings is given during the *feedback session* (Step 5). If possible, all interviewees should be present since an account is given of the findings, and the definite assignment and plan of action are also determined on the basis of their contributions. During the intake meeting, it must be agreed on with the assignment principal that all people who will be interviewed will not only receive an announcement about the coming interviews, but also an invitation to attend the feedback session. Since the orientational interviews and the analysis (Step 4) together usually do not take more than one month (at most 15 per cent of the total time allocated for the fieldwork project), the date for the feedback session must already be fixed at the intake meeting. Thus, it can be ensured that people who are important to the project will not be absent due to prior engagements. The fieldwork supervisor, whom we assume is present at the intake meeting, can then also note the date of the feedback session, as his or her presence will be highly desirable.

A good *introduction* of the student within the company is needed to give the research the necessary standing. Effective organizational change requires the company's focus on both the problem and solution. By announcing the arrival of the student who will be working on that issue with the necessary publicity, the attention that is always sought by professional consultants will be received. The manner of introduction will depend somewhat on the possibilities that are present within the company. An article with a photograph in the staff magazine is usually very effective. However, an announcement on the noticeboard or a letter to all executives to be discussed during progress meetings will also suffice. Furthermore, a personal introduction to the management team, arranged by the company coach, will be an important factor in obtaining sufficient attention and acceptance. Sometimes a student can take such an opportunity to make appointments for interviews, which obviously is very convenient.

Experience shows that companies sometimes place a particular emphasis in the introduction that the consultant or student would not find desirable. This can be prevented by offering to write a draft introduction yourself.

Example 5.2: Management announcement

Christel Herrings is going to tackle ISO-9000

Starting 1 September next, Christel Herrings, a student at the University of Hamburg (Germany), will be working here temporarily.

Christel is in the fourth year of her course at the Department of Technology Management. In the final stage of her course, she will be carrying out an eight-month fieldwork project in our company. Her assignment will be to make the preparations for our ISO certification.

As will be known, it is becoming increasingly important for the company to be ISO certified. More and more often, clients demand this certificate, even though they do not have any complaints about the quality of our products. The importance of internal procedures and methods for quality control is ever increasing.

Quality control is a task for us all. Therefore, Christel will hold interviews with all seven managers involved to canvass their ideas, wants and possibilities.

Christel will hold a presentation on her first findings for the interviewees during an MT meeting on 5 October next. In the subsequent discussion, she will also make her proposals for the definite formulation of her assignment and her plan of action.

We would ask you all to co-operate with Christel, to make her time with us as pleasant and effective as possible. She will contact the people involved shortly to fix a date for the interviews.

Peter Jensen, managing director

To: all executives for discussion during the work progress meetings

---

A *guided tour of the company* at the end of the intake meeting is advisable. Much of what has been discussed during the meeting will be confirmed when the processes are actually seen and explained. Asking questions during the tour can provide an insight into the organization and the problem to be solved.

The people in the company nearly always find it very positive when a consultant or student shows an interest in the actual processes involved.

Sometimes such a tour of the company after the intake meeting will be impossible or not very useful, due to lack of time or because the distance between the location of the meeting and the plant is too great. It is also possible that the timing may be inappropriate – for instance, because the factory is inoperative. Arrangements can then be made for a walk through the company during a subsequent visit.

List of action points

For the intake meeting the following steps need to be completed in succession:

1 Draft an agenda for the intake meeting
2 Consult with the fieldwork supervisor about the agenda and the roles of the people involved
3 Hold the intake meeting in the presence of the fieldwork supervisor
4 Take minutes of the intake meeting
5 Send the minutes to the assignment principal
6 Carry out follow-up agreements
7 Complete the relevant logbook page.

Chapter notes

[1] See also Bell (1986) on the intake/entry as the critical phase in a consultancy process.

[2] Schein (1999: 222) and Greiner and Metzger (1983: 254) stress the importance of making contact with the 'movers and shakers' of the organization. They recommend holding a meeting with the key executives who are – even if only in part – responsible for areas to which the assignment relates and could relate. This first discussion is not intended as an interview for collecting information but as an introduction. Later, it may be useful to hold another interview with members of the management team.

[3] See also Kubr (2002: 144):

> The consultant should encourage the client to do most of the talking so that he hears about the circumstances which led to the meeting and why the client considered that consulting might help him. It is well for the discussion to develop from the general situation to the particular and to focus eventually on the real issue.

[4] See also Schein (1999: 71–2, 228) for a description of the role of and interaction with the client.

Exercises for Step 2

5.1   The Clinker Ltd

Brickworks The Clinker Ltd is located in an area along the Dutch/German border that is known as something of a problem region. Unemployment there is 12 per cent.

The company's products include building bricks and clinkers for housing, paving and playgrounds. In addition, they also sell refractory stones.

A structural study with respect to the sector in which the company is active has revealed that there is overcapacity of about 30–40 per cent. Profit margins are low and pressure on prices is high.

The company is situated close to the centre of the village of Luten. The heavy lorries can only reach the site by driving through the village centre, thus causing much nuisance and resulting in protests from the villagers.

Due to the problematic character of both the region and the sector, there is much government intervention in the form of subsidies that, until now, the company has not made use of.

The market in which it operates is strongly segmented, with the result that the manufactured bricks and paving stones are hardly ever mutually interchangeable.

The Clinker Ltd is a family business that is managed by brothers Bert and Ernie Petersen. They are in charge of production and sales respectively. Eighteen months ago, Mr Jansen joined the company as assistant manager in charge of product development. The father of both managers has effectively retired. He is 60 years old and the only thing he still does for the company is maintain contacts with a number of large customers. He can still be found on the site often, but is not actively involved in day-to-day business. However, it was on his advice that Mr Jansen was taken on. It took much power of persuasion to obtain his sons' consent to this action.

Bert is the more dominant of the two brothers. He has the organization of production well under control. Ernie, on the other hand, thinks planning and organization are only necessary to a certain extent. His rule of thumb is that in business you must have the courage to strike at the right moment and that you cannot plan and organize everything in advance. Taking on the third member of the management has had little consequence with respect to workload; all three managers have an average working week of 60–70 hours.

The company has a staff of 58 in total. The following departments come under management: warehouse, production, accounting, sales, product development, and technical services.

Although, all in all, everyone within the organization has been assigned an area of responsibility, a degree of overlap some-times occurs in the execution of tasks. Moreover, the executives (management and department managers) often find it difficult to delegate tasks.

The atmosphere in management is reasonably good, but lower down the hierarchy it is less so. Everyone within the company has many informal contacts, which promotes gossip that is accentuated by the fact that they all know and criticize the ups and downs of each other's family lives, since they all live in the same small community.

The reason for calling in a student is the plan to relocate the company. The council wants the company away from the village centre and moved to an industrial estate on the outskirts of the village. This relocation raises many questions.

Mr Petersen Sr has contacted your educational institution to offer a fieldwork project. You have found this project through the bureau of fieldwork projects. A talk with Mr Petersen Sr and an external orientation that you have carried out have resulted in the above description of the company. You are now preparing your-self for the intake meeting that you will be having with the three Messrs Petersen in the presence of your fieldwork supervisor.

1 Draft the agenda for the intake meeting and give a reasoned time estimate for each item on it.
2 Design a questionnaire with ten items to indicate what you would like to learn during the meeting about the company and the fieldwork project.
3 What role do you expect your fieldwork supervisor to play during the meeting and how do you prepare your supervisor for that role?
4 Draft your own communication for your introduction, which you can send as a draft to The Clinker Ltd.
5 Who would you prefer as company coach during the project and why?

6   What are the five main problems in the relocation of and construction of a new plant for an entire company?
7   What knowledge do you need to acquire beforehand to be able to carry out this fieldwork assignment?
8   From your contacts with The Clinker Ltd you have discovered that they are not very precise in keeping appointments. How can you ensure that they will not 'forget' the date of the intake meeting?
9   Make a distinction between the acquisition meeting and the intake meeting by comparing the agendas for each meeting.
10 What requirements should a company coach meet and how can you test these during the intake meeting?

Chapter 6

Step 3: Orientational interviews

In the orientation phase, we have now come to the point where the relevant external developments, and the wants and expectations of the assignment principal, are known. Many people will now want to start working on the contract and the fieldwork assignment. As a student, however, you are still lacking several important items of information. There is no or hardly any insight into the:

- primary processes of the organization
- views of the other people involved
- organization culture
- differences and similarities in opinions about the problem and the readiness within the organization to contribute to working on a solution
- extent to which people within the company have already worked on the problem and the reason they have not been successful
- available research data
- nature and size of the consulting work to find a solution for the formulated problem
- support for the assignment and the approach.

Naturally, one can take the point of view that these matters will become apparent during the execution of the fieldwork assignment. This may well be so, but then you, as a consultant or fieldwork student, often find yourself in the middle of an area of tension, and your room to manoeuvre to clear up any misunderstandings or differences in expectations will be considerably less than at this point in the orientation phase. An example is given in Case 6.1.

Case 6.1

A consultant was asked to take on an assignment by a canning factory. During the intake meeting he met the managing director, who told him that the company had been experiencing a decline in its operating results for a number of years. After the umpteenth year of loss, he had come to the conclusion that external help was needed. He had read publications by the consultant in question on a Profit Improvement Programme, which had greatly appealed to him.

The consultant accepted the assignment and started work straight away. Soon he met some other members of the management team who rebuffed him and did not seem willing to co-operate with him.

Only at that time did it become clear to him that there was a fundamental difference of opinion between the managing director and the other managers about the course to take towards a recovery of the operating results. The manager was accused of imposing his will by hiring the consultant without any form of consultation. As a result, the consultant was seen as being in the enemy camp. All he encountered was distrust and the only thing he could do was discontinue the assignment.

A number of orientational interviews with the other members of the management team before accepting the assignment would have given an insight into the existing conflict much sooner. Perhaps then he would have been able to bridge the gap between both parties and make the assignment workable.

There always remain questions that have not been answered sufficiently after the intake meeting, as well as facts and circumstances that are still unclear. An orientational study before accepting an assignment is therefore very advisable. It involves a perspective and risk analysis at a time when any risks and possibilities that come to light can still be influenced. An organization is a joint venture of groups and individuals who agree on some points but totally disagree on others. As a student, you can end up in the middle of conflicting interests. In order to help effectively, it is desirable to obtain the best possible insight into the relations as early in the process as possible. This will give you the opportunity to gear your approach to the existing situation.[1]

This research is only short and concise. This step – the orientational interviews – should not evolve imperceptibly into in-depth research. It is important to make a distinction that is clearly visible to the company between orientational interviews contributing to careful *contracting* on the one hand and in-depth research as part of the *execution of the assignment* on the other.

Misunderstandings about what still can or cannot be regarded as orientational interviews can easily arise (see Case 6.2).

Case 6.2

Owing to circumstances, a consultant decided to hold about 20 orientational interviews. Due to the busy schedules of the people involved, it took him about two months to complete all these interviews. When he finally gave feedback on his findings to the principal, thinking he could still negotiate some elements of the assignment, he encountered opposition and incomprehension. The principal assumed that the discussion on the formulation of the assignment that had taken place two months earlier had already been concluded – albeit verbally. The fact that the consultant had already done so much work only strengthened that impression.

In our experience, about five to ten orientational interviews, with a report of findings within a month at most after the start, offer a reasonable starting point. To prevent any misunderstanding it is advisable to mention during each conversation that the interview is exploratory and contributes to the final contract.

This attitude influences the nature of the questions in the orientational interviews. They must be *exploratory* and *inventorial*, contrary to the questions in the in-depth research, where one should know all the ins and outs to obtain *problem- and solution-directed* information.

What we mean by exploratory and inventorial will become clear when we look at the example of a completed checklist (Table 6.1) concerning a number of orientational interviews that

Table 6.1
Example of a completed logbook page for Step 3

Checklist – Step 3: Orientational interviews	
Questions	**Answers**
1　What different problem descriptions emerge from the interviews?	• Declining market • Too expensive machinery • Weak project management
2　What different problem formulations emerge from the interviews?	• Developing a brochure • Efficiency improvement • Training project managers
3　In which directions does one suggest looking for a solution?	• Developing a brochure • Efficiency improvement • Training project managers
4　What conditions for solving the problem are mentioned?	• Replacement of current managing director • Claim on supplies to sister companies within the concern
5　Which information is required but not available?	• Turnover per product/market combination • Insight into competition
6　Has every respondent been invited to the feedback meeting?	• Yes, with the exception of the administrator, since management has forbidden his presence
7　What was the result of the final interview with the assignment principal?	• See item 6 • Understanding for various views • Own position as managing director is non-discussable
8　On which data can project planning be based?	• Number of interviews • Number of competitors • Number of (prospective) customers to be approached
9　Which documentation is available at the moment?	• Strategic plan, organizational chart, project management system • Four annual accounts, plan layout
10　Remarks	

were held in a machine works. The machine works in question was not doing well, but there were differences of opinion about the cause. As a result, a remedial approach could not be agreed upon. Furthermore, the relations between the managing director and the other members of the management team were strained.

This description of the situation shows how things can go wrong if a student or consultant starts working on the in-depth research immediately. It is true that it is not easy to arrive at an approach that is supported by all in such a situation. However, now at least the situation can be taken into account and, if necessary, the project can be discontinued before too much time has been spent on it.

Primarily, one should get to know the mutual relations and opinions during the orientational interviews.

In-depth analyses of the problem are not required at this point. At a later stage, after agreement on the final assignment has been reached with the assignment principal, the parties involved will have to be interviewed once again about the details of the problem and possible solutions.

The questions asked in the orientational interviews are exploratory and inventorial, but also have a change-directed aspect. Interviewing a number of people who are involved in the problem situation within a company has an activating and mobilizing effect. It kills two birds with one stone: the consultant or student obtains information that is indispensable for the execution of an effective consulting process and the interviewees at the company can express their concerns and opinions, and feel that they are not being left out of the proceedings.

Provided they are carried out well, these orientational interviews will help to start the change process in the organization, and the necessary bond of trust between the parties involved and the consultant or student will be brought about. This will work best in individual interviews. Within the confidentiality of such a conversation, respondents are often also willing to talk more openly about the atmosphere within the organization, the co-operation with colleagues, and the good and bad habits of the boss, the secretary or themselves. This is often of the utmost importance for a good understanding of the background to the problem. Although this type of sensitive information should be dealt with in strict confidence, it is possible to consider it in a very responsible manner. For instance, one should think very carefully before deciding to place two rivals in the same work group.

Students often disregard the aspect of this bond of trust that can be created by means of individual interviews. As fieldwork supervisors we have often encountered situations where students, in their zeal to consult (too) many people in their orientation, used questionnaires or group interviews. After the previous discussion it will be clear that such a method is undesirable at this stage, since the desired side-effects will be lost.

Topics for discussion

To support the correct method of questioning, a list is given below of topics for discussion that usually come up during the interviews. We will briefly discuss the subjects mentioned on the list.

The most important topics for discussion for orientational interviews are:

- Verification/adjustment of the introduction
- Contents of the function; career patter
- Process charts – production flows, organizational chart, connection and co-operation between the departments, units and functions that are of importance to the assignment
- The nature of involvement in the problem
- Views on the problem and its backgrounds/causes
- Views on the roles of other people involved
- Views on and contribution to the solution of the problem
- The reason why a solution has not been found/ implemented
- How will the consultant/student be able to help?
- What is the necessary information? Where can it be obtained? In what form?
- Requests for documentation
- Confirmation of the invitation to the feedback session.

Verification/adjustment of the introduction

When the student has been introduced properly, the people to be interviewed will have been informed of the student's arrival. However, it is advisable that the student verifies at the beginning whether the people involved have been informed correctly and fully. If necessary, additional information needs to be given or false impressions need to be corrected.

Communication within an organization is not always perfect. People may have been absent when the message was sent, the message might still be lying in a pile of unread mail or incorrect addresses may have been used. Even when the message has been received, it is advisable to start by repeating its contents. Thus, a mutual starting point is formed and an additional, personal introduction often acts as a good way to break the ice.

Contents of the function; career pattern

Enquiring about the function and career pattern offers the interviewee an opportunity to introduce himself or herself. It is important here to spend extra time on the aspects affecting the problem area, such as (co)responsibilities, special experience or knowledge, insight from earlier positions and relations with other responsible managers.

Verification and fine-tuning of process charts

During the intake meeting, as a rule the assignment principal will have described the processes in the organization (production flows, organizational chart, etc.). When the student is holding the orientational interviews, he or she will probably already be in possession of documents describing the various processes and organizational connections.

However, for three reasons it can be very useful to also enquire about the organization of the relevant processes during the orientational interviews. In the successive interviews you will:

- be obtaining an increasingly more complete picture of the relevant processes
- be able to link individuals to tasks and responsibilities
- get a feeling for the differences that nearly always exist between the official and actual relationships.

The nature of involvement in the problem

Continuing to ask questions always gives insight into the importance the interviewee attaches to the fact that the student is tackling the problem. In addition, it reveals to what extent the problem is important enough to the interviewee that he or she, if asked, will be willing to co-operate with its potential solution. The greater the personal interest in a good solution, the greater the commitment of the person involved.

Views on the problem and its backgrounds/causes

Hardly ever do all the people involved have the same perspective on what is happening. It is exactly this lack of a mutual opinion about the nature and causes of problems that leads to stagnation of the problem-solving process. For this reason, it is important to the student to focus sharply on the subtle distinctions in the various views on the problem and the causes that lie behind them. By continuing to ask questions, one should try to get as complete a picture as possible.

Views on the roles of other people involved

Most problems that require a solution involve the competence of people in various positions. This creates a certain mutual dependence when trying to find a solution. If one person takes the initiative and another does not co-operate, the process will come to a halt. Sometimes people wait for each other, resulting in no action at all. To be able to develop a good approach as a student, insight into these mutual dependencies is necessary. This picture becomes clear by asking every interviewee his or her view on the roles of the other people involved.

Views on and contribution to the solution of the problem

Usually, attempts have already been made to find a solution. A serious problem will activate people. This is shown by:

- The agendas and discussions in the management team
- The establishment of a work group
- Internal memos and correspondence
- Previous hiring of outsiders (consultants, market researchers, experts)
- Mutual consultations between the people involved
- Decisions taken
- Instructions given
- Overtime worked to fight the causes of the bottleneck.

By asking what has been done so far to solve the problem and asking for the available documentation, if any, the desired insight will be gained. This can certainly be surprising. One of us experienced a situation where an interviewee took a complete report out of a cabinet that he had written himself. In it, a clear indication was given of what he thought was wrong and had to be done. To our question of why these proposals had never been implemented, the employee replied that management had not shared his view and therefore had not been willing to accept his approach. The problem had remained unsolved.

Why has no solution been found/implemented?

The answers to this question should reveal what is holding the company back in finding a solution to the problem. In many cases, people have differing views on this subject. Armed with this insight, the student is often faced with the challenge of addressing a possible dilemma with a new approach. Careful questioning and meticulous recording of the various explanations are therefore required.

How will the student be able to help?

We assume the student has the ambition to support the organization in the approach to the problem at hand. Of course, he or she will have to determine his or her own independent consulting position. Knowing the various expectations can help in this process. For instance, when it appears from the interviews that a number of reports have been written without being used, the next report will almost certainly be greeted with scepticism. Such a situation therefore requires an original and different approach.

What is the necessary information? Where is it available? In what form?

This question serves to enable you to make an estimate of the extent of research necessary. When market information is needed that is not available (in the right form), market research may have to be incorporated in the plan of action.

Not having the necessary data at your disposal usually results in a loss of time. It is one of the most common reasons for overrunning the schedule in a fieldwork project. Therefore, a series of orientational interviews must provide clarity on this point. This does not, of course, solve the planning problems, but if it is recognized in good time that this forms a bottleneck, it can be found whether the company may still be able to take measures to obtain the necessary data. In any case, the organization's expectations of the results that will be feasible in the period of the fieldwork project can still be altered.

Incidentally, a strange misunderstanding often occurs on this point. If students encounter a lack of information in the problem area, they quite often tend to take the position that they are therefore faced with an insoluble problem. There is no data on the market, customer satisfaction and turnover, and therefore they think they cannot go any further. What they do not realize enough is that a lack of data can actually uncover an important clue to the problem. Many activities within an organization get out of hand because they are not sufficiently controlled. Control involves having measurement points for the course of the activity, determining standards and norms, registering measurement data on the actual course, and adjusting any deviations from the norm. Establishing a lack of data leads to the conclusion that this control cycle does not exist or is not functioning efficiently.

It is at such a moment that the student should realize that the design and incorporation of a control cycle could be one of his or her important contributions to solving the problem. With this knowledge, it is wise not to lose any throughput time because of lack of data, but to start gathering the data as soon as possible. Usually, the employees are then willing to keep records of daily stock numbers, percentage of rejects and the like, based on clear instructions. So, if you as a student need the data a little later, you will then have these records at your disposal.

Requesting documentation

During the interviews, it will often be assumed that relevant information has been recorded. A summary of the possible sources of information was given under the heading 'Views on and contribution to the solution of the problem'. In general, it is disruptive when the interview has to be stopped repeatedly because the interviewee has to go and look for something. It is better to arrange for documentation to be available for reference during the interview, but to postpone the actual handing over of these documents until the end of the interview. To ensure that no important sources of information are overlooked, it is advisable that the student takes note of the documents that were discussed during the interview.

Confirmation of the invitation for the feedback session

During the intake meeting with the assignment principal it will already have been arranged that all interviewees will be present during the feedback session – Step 5. It is important to check whether this invitation has indeed reached the interviewees and whether they have noted the date in their diaries. If necessary, they can then still be invited. It can also heighten their interest by pointing out the importance of the meeting.

Processing and completing the interviews

As the most important topics for discussion for the orientational interviews have been discussed, we now focus on the question of how the results can be processed.

To process the interviews correctly in Step 4, Analysis, an effective record of the subjects discussed is required. For someone who is not experienced at holding interviews, this is not an easy task. One must look the respondent in the eye and listen very attentively in order to be able to ask follow-up questions after an answer is given, if necessary, while at the same time also making notes. Usually, this problem is solved by only writing down key words or short sentences during the interview, on the basis of which a full report is written immediately after the interview. Then, the context of the short notes will still be fresh in the memory.

It is not always necessary to give an interviewee a copy of the report of the meeting. During the feedback session, interviewees are shown the results of the entire round of interviews. The individual input of the respondents in this report will be partially blurred and in any case will have been incorporated anonymously. The people at the meeting can then freely and openly discuss the assignment without being pinned down on their individual statements.

To be able to process the interview reports efficiently it is useful to start each new interview topic on a new page of the notebook. They are then easier to sort later – this is called 'stacking' (see Step 4).

Until now, we have assumed that the group of respondents was selected during the intake meeting. In practice, it often happens that during the interviews names come up of people involved who are not yet on the list that was drawn up earlier. This can lead to an adjustment of this list. The best way of dealing with this is to make a reasoned proposal to the assignment principal to interview these people as well, provided the total number does not become too large. Usually, consent will be given to do so, unless there are weighty arguments against it.

Through the intake meeting, the work in the consulting project started with the assignment principal. At the end of the series of interviews, it is advisable to have a closing interview with the assignment principal. This provides the opportunity to ask questions that so far remain unanswered and to give a general impression of the first findings. Moreover, the agreements can be gone over once again with respect to the feedback session.

Interview technique

Finally, we would like to discuss the subject of interview technique. In most courses, some form of interview training is incorporated. For this reason, we confine ourselves here to some remarks about the value of the answers obtained during the interviews.[2]

The interviewer has certain intentions in holding the interview: he or she wants to understand what is actually going on in the organization, what the person on the other side of the table thinks of the problem, and so on. Here, each interviewer has at least two fundamental problems: does he or she understand what the respondent is saying and can he or she rely on the truth of what the respondent is saying?

In your interview strategy, you as interviewer have to take both these problems into account. You have to ask yourself in advance how you can hold your interview in such a way that you will end up with sufficiently valid and trustworthy results.

Not understanding what the respondent is saying can be the result of a difference in knowledge on the subject of the interview. The respondent answers the exploratory questions of the interviewer. The interviewer explores what in many respects is very obvious to the respondent. Students in particular find it very difficult at first to continue to ask questions when they do not (fully) understand what the respondent is telling them. They then make the mistake of thinking that any additional questions will be regarded as ignorance. Some interviewees will realize that the student does not yet understand the company lingo. As a consultant or student you do not have to see that solely as a disadvantage. It offers you a legitimate reason to ask questions the people involved may not have asked themselves for a very long time. This implies that it is advisable to immediately ask for further explanation about things the respondent says that you do not understand. Those who think they will understand it later when working out the notes will almost always be disappointed. One way to gain understanding of what has been said neutrally and without losing face is to sum up the part you *did* understand: 'So, if I understand you correctly, you mean . . .' Without fail, virtually every respondent will fill in any gaps that come to light. If later you start to feel uncertain about what the respondent actually meant, it is advisable to contact him or her and ask for elucidation of that specific point.

The veracity of what the respondent is saying relates to the question of whether the respondent is telling you things without any distortion or embellishment. As interviewer, you can almost never really check whether respondents are telling the 'truth'. They can have different reasons for slightly altering the facts:

■ To be friendly. The respondent does not want to offend the interviewer. For instance, he does not reply because he does not want to reveal that the question does not relate to his situation, or he replies but actually does not know enough of the facts to give an answer.

■ Socially desirable behaviour. The respondent wants to give a good impression and colours the answers slightly to fit what he thinks is expected – for instance, by the boss or colleagues.

■ Distortion of time. When questions are about facts from the past, often things get distorted. There is a change in sequence, or the respondent's role and those of other people are remembered differently from what actually occurred.

■ Suppression. Every respondent has delicate or sensitive subjects that they would rather not discuss (again). This can relate to painful memories of responsibilities that could not be fulfilled, promotion opportunities that were missed, or conflicts.

The interviewer must be prepared for these eventualities. As soon as the interviewer gets the impression that the respondent is not completely telling the truth or is distorting or embellishing it, it is best to keep on asking questions. A simple, but often very effective, way to continue questioning is to ask for the answer to be made more concrete: 'Could you give an example?' 'When you say this mistake is often made, could you tell me how many times exactly?' 'If you say that those customers have complained very often, where have these complaints been recorded or who has heard them also?'

This also brings us to the point of the importance of quantification of statements. In each interview, there are usually times where quantifying questions can be asked, such as how often, how much, how many times, how large. For example:

- The machines break down quite often – how often?
- The boss should not badger us – how often does he do that?
- Complaints are pouring in – how many on average per day/week?
- There is much breakage during the production of the biscuits – how much in percentage of production?
- We work ourselves to death – how short and few are the breaks, how many hours of overtime?

Often, these possibilities for quantification are hidden behind casual remarks. It is therefore important to be very attentive when using such remarks to ask for quantitative data. Given the difficulty students have in working this way, we advise you to judge yourself on the number of quantitative items of information per interview. In addition, you can make a habit of noting the desirable quantitative data behind each question when you are preparing for an interview.

Why is insight into figures so important? Because it provides a definitive picture. The statement 'The machines break down at least once every day' gives a much more spectacular image than 'Each month, the machines tend to break down once'. Both images can lie hidden behind the statement: 'The machines break down quite often.'

Another reason to seek to obtain insight into figures is the possibility of verifying the uniformity of opinions and perceptions by comparing the various statements. Many organizational problems remain unsolved because people have different insights into a problem. This causes differences in urgency and thus in readiness to change.

Finally, we mention the manager's perception of the situation as a plea for support of statements by numerical data. To manage is to control by measurable quantities. We know the parts of each controlled process: determination of the measuring points, zero-point measurement, setting tasks, measurement of the results achieved, comparison with the tasks set and adjustment, if necessary. Someone who lives and works in such a world of measurements will put more value on statements like 'We have to reduce the number of customer complaints from ten to two per month' than 'The number of customer complaints must be reduced'.

Based on all these considerations it will have become clear that a feedback presentation with the necessary support of numerical data will be considerably stronger and will increase the credibility of the approach to the follow-up strategy.

List of action points

This step is again completed by a summary of the activities that need to be carried out consecutively at this stage:

1 Make a list of points of attention for the interviews
2 Verify agreements
3 Prepare the 'stacking' of the outcomes of the interviews
4 Interview and increase insight into quantifiable facts and circumstances
5 Take notes during the interviews
6 Complete the relevant logbook pages.

Chapter notes

[1] See Schein (1999: 228–9), who stresses the importance of orientational interviews. He sees these interviews as a means for the consultant to introduce himself or herself to those members of the organization who are important for the assignment and to obtain information about the organization, the problem and the people in the organization.

[2] See Emans (2004).

Exercises for Step 3

6.1 Revision of the budgeting system for a car recycling company

1   From the organizational chart of a company that man-ufactures high-tech machinery for the car industry (Figure 6.1) identify with whom (ten people at most) you would certainly want to hold an orientational inter-view, if the assignment were the revision of the budgeting system.

2   Who do you expect to be present during the intake meeting (two people at most)?

3   Draft your list of questions (20 questions at most) for the orientational interviews.

4   Indicate what knowledge you are lacking to carry out the assignment.

5   During the series of orientational interviews it appears that four of the respondents you had arranged interviews with will not be available after all. It is impossible to find

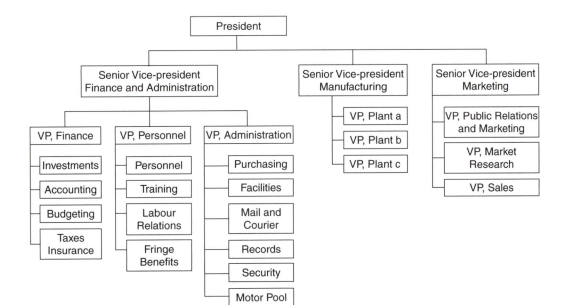

Figure 6.1
Organizational chart of a high-tech machinery manufacturing firm.

new dates before the date that has already been fixed for the feedback session. How do you solve this problem?

6   During the orientational interviews, a number of respondents comment very negatively on the Finance Vice-President and your intended assignment. How do you deal with that situation?

Chapter 7

Step 4: The analysis

In the analysis stage, the information that has been obtained from the external orientation, the intake meeting, the study of documents and the orientational interviews is arranged and interpreted in order to make final agreements on the formulation of the problem. These agreements will be made in Step 5 – the feedback session. The main subjects in the feedback presentation act as convenient headings for the analysis. The main points in this presentation are:

- Relevant findings – opinions and process descriptions
- Proposal for definitive formulation of the problem and assignment
- Indication of the importance attached to the solution of the problem
- Specification of the way in which the student can contribute to solving the problem
- Plan of action.

Of course, much more information will become available than can be covered by these points. However, to avoid overload in the presentation, it is advisable to use these key points as a basis on which to work. The presentation itself will offer the possibility to give some more information around the key questions.

The so-called stacking method is a good way of generating a good overview from the pile of interview reports.[1] Figure 7.1 illustrates the steps to be taken using this method. First, the interview reports and summaries of the study of the documents are coded (by theme and respondent). Thus, on each theme, insight is obtained into the available data. Based on this, the subjects

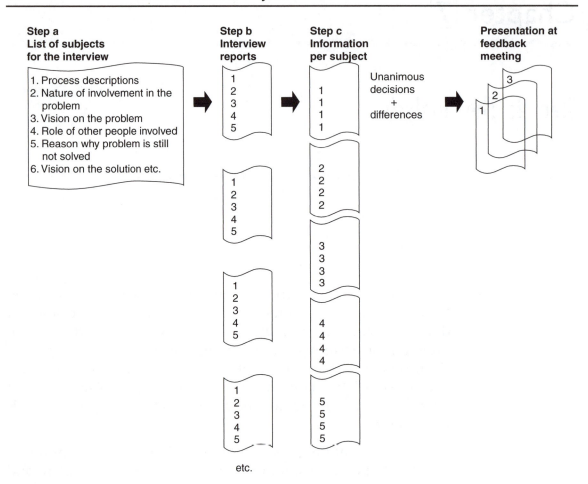

Figure 7.1
Stacking of research results.

one wants to discuss in the presentation can be worked out on transparency films.

We once again underline that students have to anticipate the data processing that will follow later, when preparing the list of subjects for the interviews (see Step 3). In practice, we have seen students lose much time because they collected data in a rather unstructured manner and subsequently almost could not see the wood for the trees.

The method of stacking involves:

a Making a list of main questions for the interviews; these are the questions that have to be asked during each interview.

b   For each respondent, making an interview report in which the answers to the main questions are worked out in the same sequence.

c   Collecting similar answers to the main questions.

d   For each main question, making the following analysis – where do the answers match and where do they differ? These are the building blocks for the presentation at the feedback session.

To explain what should have been achieved at the end of the analysis, we have completed the checklist questions for this step for a dairy factory that was faced with a relatively high level of absenteeism. The answers to the questions shown in Table 7.1 were derived from the analysis of the information that had been gathered about and within the organization.

By means of a number of questions from the checklist, we will further examine some of the work that is done in the analysis.

Description of the processes

An important part of the analysis consists of a systematic description of the relevant operations. Students must quickly obtain an overview of these processes and the related tasks and responsibilities in order to become a serious discussion partner to the people who are used to talking about problems and bottlenecks in the company in terms directly related to these processes. We advise always making a flow chart.[2]

Differences of opinion

In the orientational interviews, respondents have been asked to describe the problem, what they think is causing it, etc. The objective of the analysis is to reveal the similarities and differences between the respondents' views. This is necessary because the progress of the consulting project requires that consensus is reached on the nature of the problem, the assignment for the student and the plan of action. The student provides the input for this point of discussion. In the case of the dairy factory, it appeared that everyone agreed that the level of absenteeism was

Table 7.1
Example of a completed logbook page for Step 4

Checklist – Step 4: Analysis	
Questions	**Answers**
1 What is the schematic view of the company's primary process or business unit in which the fieldwork project is carried out?	• Flow chart of the relevant processes
2 On which points do the interviewees hold different views? Describe the differences	• Absenteeism due to working conditions versus absenteeism due to merger issue
3 Which methods of analysis did you use?	• Process analysis and statistical analysis
4 What should be the result of the feedback meeting?	• Consensus on the problem • Confirmation of the agreement
5 Which proposal on a final assignment formulation emerges from the orientation carried out up to now?	• A decrease in the level of absenteeism from 10% to 7% within one year
6 Who should be invited to join the platform group?	• The managing director, manager and HR manager
7 What should be the further plan of action for the research?	• Analysis of control of absenteeism • Work satisfaction research • Comparison with similar companies
8 What is the outline of the presentation for the feedback meeting?	• See presentation
9 Which specific problems with respect to the execution of the assignment will have to be solved during the feedback meeting?	• Obtaining the co-operation of the works council
10 Remarks	

too high, but opinions differed on what caused this level to be so high and on the urgency of the research.

What should be the result of the feedback session?

In question 4, a number of factors play a part. First, students decide for themselves whether it is possible to formulate an acceptable assignment. Important criteria for this decision are whether the student can add sufficient value to the solution of the problem and whether the level of implementation of the assignment is high enough. If there is considerable doubt with respect to one of these criteria, it is better to abandon the assignment. Possible considerations are: lack of necessary knowledge on the subject; insufficient external management support (for instance, from a parent company abroad); insufficient leeway for the student to carry out the assignment as it should be done; insufficient supervision from the company, or imminent problems of continuity in the company; doubts about whether the learning process will meet the requirements of the course.

In the analysis of the results of the various explorational activities, students must cast a critical eye at the project in this respect. When there is doubt, they should confer with their fieldwork supervisor before the feedback session takes place.

In Case 7.1 a description is given of a situation in which it was decided to stop proceedings.

Case 7.1

During the orientational interviews with a manufacturer of industrial pumps, where the subject of research was to be the cost price calculation, a student learned from various employees that the company was in very bad shape financially. A bankruptcy in the next few months could not even be ruled out. It was considered doubtful whether he would be able to finish the project in these circumstances. In consultation with his fieldwork supervisor, it was decided to discuss the matter with the assignment principal. The assignment principal could not guarantee that the project would be completed. Therefore, by mutual agreement, they decided to end the fieldwork project.

The second thing the feedback session must provide is a good starting point for the execution of the fieldwork assignment. Preconditions must be:

- Consensus of opinion on the formulation of the problem
- General acceptance of the formulation of the assignment and the plan of action (project proposal).

Often, it is taken too much for granted that this will all be in order. It is better to discuss this subject explicitly during the feedback session, to prevent later disappointments or misunderstandings. This will be discussed further in Step 5.

Platform group

Question 6 of the checklist refers to a platform group. This may need some elucidation. During the execution of the assignment, the consultant or student occasionally has the need for some confidential internal consultations, besides the formal deliberations with the assignment principal or the management team. This need arises particularly when there are problems with obtaining the right information, when making important decisions on the execution of the assignment, or testing the first ideas on possible solutions. Of course, the company supervisor will be the first person to consult. However, a small platform group or sounding board consisting of the most important sponsors of the project – including the company supervisor – will give the consultations more breadth and support to get the selected process accepted and subsequently implemented.

It is necessary to decide in consultation with your company supervisor during the analysis whether such a platform group can be of use and, if so, how this group should be made up. The interviews provide an excellent basis to determine who is most willing to make a case for successful execution of the assignment. The proposal to establish a platform group can be made and accepted during the feedback session.[3]

Further plan of action

To be able to answer question 7 in the logbook, 'What should the plan of action for the research look like?', conclusions have to be reached. The most important conclusion is a diagnosis of the problem at hand. During the intake meeting an assignment will have been formulated, and five to ten interviews held to verify the correctness and usefulness of, and support for, the formulation of the problem. The available documentation will have been studied. All these actions were also undertaken to enable you to form your own opinion of the problem that you think it is best to tackle. This should not always be the problem originally formulated in the intake meeting. Many factors can cause differences, as seen in the following examples:

- 'The investigation and improvement of the organizational processes' was changed to 'the preparation of the company for ISO certification', since that was the actual objective.
- 'To decrease costs by 10 per cent' was limited, due to time constraints, as 'to decrease the costs by 5 per cent by means of contracting out of activities'.
- 'To improve the structure of the organization' was made more specific, 'to improve the co-operation between the various departments to raise customer satisfaction to a score of 8 or higher'. This appeared to be the underlying problem, and also proved to have more support than a change in structure.
- After the orientational interviews, 'to carry out market research' was amended as 'to increase the market share by 10 per cent in one year'. This was the reason for the market research in the first place.

All these examples show that a critical assessment of the original problem formulation often gives a better and more fitting assignment. The differences can be summarized as:

- Broadening or narrowing the assignment (market research, contracting out)
- Making the objective more concrete and measurable (ISO)
- Finding another way to tackle the problem, because that will find more support (communication).

The last example reveals another interesting aspect of fieldwork, namely that there are often many different ways to obtain the same result. In this case, it is evidently the generally recognized problem that customer satisfaction is suffering from the unco-ordinated way in which the departments involved are functioning. The intended result of the assignment is higher customer satisfaction; the means is better co-operation. Obviously, during the intake meeting the managing director felt that the best way to improve this co-operation was by means of a change in structure, and that is why he agreed to that assignment. However, co-operation between departments can also be improved by training, by increasing bonuses dependent on customer satisfaction for everyone, by changes in management, etc. In the orientational interviews there was consensus on the problem (too low customer satisfaction) and the cause (co-operation), but the respondents would not commit themselves to a change in structure as a pretext for improvement. Consultants and students can best concentrate on the problem and causes during the orientation phase. Keeping a sufficient distance from all kinds of ideas for solutions will give them the leeway to form their own independent views. During the in-depth research, there will be opportunities to expand upon the diagnosis and thus find the most favourable solution alternatives.

Apart from determining the diagnosis of the problem and the assignment, the approach to the research should also contain a global plan of action. In the presentation during the feedback session, the sequence 'problem–cause–plan of action' can be presented and discussed in terms of their mutual relationship. When consensus is reached, it will immediately clear a path for the entire plan of action for the in-depth research.

So, how can research methods be applied to solve an organizational problem? An organizational problem such as 'a high level of absenteeism' is formulated in too abstract a way to be able to promote any research activity. To be able to do so first requires division of the problem into subproblems that can each be translated into research that needs to be done. The question now is how to go about making this division.

We consider it a challenge to incorporate some experiences in this book that can help students to tackle problems by drawing up workable plans of action. For this, we have selected one assignment and given six possible methods of analysis from which to form a plan of action. This best illustrates the differences and similarities in methodology. The most obvious way for students to proceed is to use their own professional knowledge. We have often observed how students in the analysis stage seem to forget what they learned during their studies when attempting to relate this knowledge to their fieldwork projects. Time and again, they find it difficult to apply generic knowledge to a specific case that is always slightly different from what is described in the literature.

However, this is required to give an analysis sufficient intrinsic depth. Questions to ask in this regard are:

■ Which key words relate to the specific character of the problem formulation? Try to find these key words in the indices of textbooks and literature search engines.

- If references are found, pay particular attention to the definitions that are used, the causes that are given for the problem in question, the solutions that are suggested, and any specific circumstances that may be of importance in finding an appropriate solution.
- How did others tackle the same problem? Look in the library archives – for instance, of your own educational establishment – for reports on earlier fieldwork projects.

Such an exploration will provide a basis for the design of various scenarios. We will now show some of these here for an assignment aiming to bring down the level of absenteeism.

The assignment is to bring down the 12 per cent level of absenteeism to the branch average of 5 per cent. The execution of this assignment will be demonstrated by means of the following approaches.

1. Cause and effect analysis (CEA)

In this approach the first question is: What might be the possible causes for absenteeism? While you are brainstorming you could, for instance, think of the following:

- Inadequate control of absence
- Poor working conditions
- Low work motivation
- No medical examination when hiring staff
- The wrong measurement system, giving a false comparison with branch data.

Then the plan of action consists of researching these possible causes and finding a solution based on the results obtained.[4]

2. Process analysis

The first question in process analysis is: How does the process giving this percentage of absenteeism work? The process description could contain the following:

- Department managers keep lists of absentees
- Employees report sick to the Personnel Department, which keeps a daily list and forwards this to its Safety, Health and Welfare Service each day

- No action is taken when work is resumed within one week
- After one week of absence, the company doctor of the Safety, Health and Welfare Service makes a house call
- The company doctor visits the Personnel Department within two days.

Based on this analysis, a first idea can be formed regarding the need for further action. For instance, a notable point here is the one-week waiting period, which can easily lead to many unjustified short periods of absence.

3. Develop a measuring and control system

The basic question to be answered using this approach is: How can the aspect that needs improving be made measurable and controllable? This may result in the following activities:

- Definition of the concept of absenteeism due to illness as it is used in the branch
- Determination of the time of measurement, the measurement point, measuring unit, and beginning and end of the absence period.

4. Quantitative analysis

If sufficient information is available, the data can be analysed. The main idea is that such an approach will give an insight into the directions one can look for solutions. The analysis may contain:

- Patterns of periods – day, week, month, year
- Duration and cause of absence, and their possible relationship
- Age, sex, seniority, population group
- Absence by function, department, location
- Connections with medical reports
- Connections with attending company doctors from the Safety, Health and Welfare Service.

Based on these analyses, the research may lead to possible concentrations of absenteeism.

5. Standard checklist or work method

The starting point in this approach is that successful approaches developed elsewhere are also applicable in the company where one is carrying out the fieldwork project. This gives the following plan of action:

- Study of the literature, other fieldwork reports, other companies, and Safety, Health and Welfare Services on applicable checklists/methods to battle absenteeism
- Diagnosis by means of the selected checklist
- Analysis of the differences found between the checklist and the existing approach
- Finding improvements or deriving these from the standards.

The rest of the plan of action is largely determined by the nature and extent of the differences found.

6. Organization diagnosis

This will be useful if the orientational interviews have revealed that absenteeism is only a symptom of a more general problem. The activities may involve the following:

- Selection of a broad company diagnosis including absenteeism
- Extensive screening of the company by means of the selected method
- Follow-up actions, based on the results, with a sensible establishment of priorities.

In the end, absenteeism will be tackled by an unexpected line of approach – for instance, by settling a discussion about plans to make (part of) the company independent, which was causing much unrest amongst the employees.

The best approach is to develop a specific plan of action for the assignment, which is derived from and founded on generic knowledge in the field of the problem in question. Should this also produce an original process or approach, the research can contribute not only to the intended solution of the assignment, but also to an increase in knowledge in this field. To show how (elements of) the approaches that were described can be used in fieldwork assignments, we describe three examples derived from the practice of fieldwork projects.

Examples of fieldwork projects

1. Privatization of a general and technical services department

Activities:

- a Describing the package of services
- b Identifying the target groups
- c Identifying the competitive contractors
- d Carrying out market research among target groups and competitors
- e Redefining the offer of services in user terms
- f Designing a marketing plan and estimating the operating costs
- g Canvassing a limited trial market
- h Establishing the organizational, legal and financial requirements for independent operation
- i Evaluating the market test and implementing the organizational, legal and financial requirements
- j Initiating the status of an independent company.

This example is reminiscent of the process analysis of a privatization.

2. Increasing customer satisfaction for a company of precision mechanics

Activities:

- a Developing a measurement system for customer satisfaction
- b Carrying out a zero-point measurement among customers
- c Establishing the prescribed tasks for the measuring points (norms)
- d Determining points for improvement

     e   Assigning (allocating) the various actions for improvement to the people responsible

     f   Periodic measurement of progress

     g   Adjusting (speeding up, slowing down, changing, stabilizing) the actions for improvement.

In this approach, clear use is made of the measurement and control system method.

3. Preventing delays in improvement projects in a graphical engineering industry

Activities:

     a   Determining the exact delays by means of a trend analysis of the lead times

     b   Identifying possible causes of delays

     c   Analysing the influence of these causes on the measured delays

     d   Proposing improvements that can be implemented immediately

     e   Implementing the improvements.

In this example, elements of the numerical analysis approach can be observed in activity a. The CEA method can be recognized in the other activities.

Incidentally, these examples once again show that Step 4 can only result in a global plan of action. However, it is sufficient to indicate at the feedback session which types of research activity will lead to an acceptance of the proposed assignment formulation. The detailed plan of action will only follow in Step 6.

Students often tend to take a research model from the literature that fits their subject to a certain extent, and blindly follow the activities indicated by this model in their plan of action. Sometimes teachers stimulate this approach on the principle of 'learning to put theory into practice', but it is not very customer oriented. From the viewpoint of the assignment principal, it is incomprehensible that after a broad orientation in the field, as described above, a standard approach is suggested that could have been brought up immediately.

Work models from the literature can certainly be of use, but what matters is the way in which they are used. First, a designed-to-measure plan of action has to be made, recognizable to the assignment principal and based on the conclusions that were drawn in the previous step. Subsequently, for each activity or group of activities, it can be found whether there is an appropriate work method from the literature that can be applied in the execution of the activity/activities.

In any event, a certain degree of orientation on the relevant literature at this stage is certainly necessary. Sometimes, a proper literature study even forms part of the final assessment. This study can have various dimensions. One is the sector in which the assignment company operates. Suppose you are carrying out a project in the sector of sanitary appliances; it would be sensible to study some of the production technology.

Another starting point for a literature study may be the nature of the problem that is being tackled. If you have to start working on a business plan for a new product, there is much information to be found on business planning in the literature, if you have not yet encountered it in courses or textbooks.

Definite assignment formulation

Question 5 in the checklist deals with definite formulation of the assignment. During the acquisition and/or intake meeting, a formulation was given of the problem area that needs to be worked on. At that time, the student did not have enough specific knowledge of the organization to be able to form his or her own idea of the problem. However, after the orientational interviews that knowledge is available, making a critical redefinition and specification possible. This is now explained by means of the following example.

Suppose the initial assignment was formulated as: 'carry out research into absences due to illness'.

After an exploration of the external and internal situations, the definite assignment formulation might be:

- Identify the causes of the current level of absence of 10 per cent
- Check whether the sector's average level of absenteeism of 7 per cent is also attainable for this company

■ Develop a coherent system to bring the level of absence back to the sector average
■ Test this system by means of a pilot in the refrigeration department
■ Pass on the acquired knowledge to the other departments within the company.

This example illustrates how all sorts of facts that have become known about the company can be applied in designing the plan of action:

■ The company has a 3 per cent higher absenteeism than its competitors. There is a difference of opinion on the causes of the high level of absence; only by finding out what is really going on can all parties involved be aligned.
■ The company has had some bad experiences with ad hoc measures. The works council fears that this will once again be the outcome. The consensus is that a coherent system is called for.
■ Absenteeism is highest in the refrigeration department. In that department's discussions of progress it has come to light that people are very willing to participate in the research. In their opinion they are too often reproached unjustly by management and colleagues from other departments about the high level of absence.
■ In previous projects, end reports had been made without implementation ever taking place. In this case, they want an assurance that attention will be paid to this subject.

Our preference for assignment formulations with concrete, measurable final results will also have become clear. Assignment principals are attracted to fieldwork projects with levels of quality that reach far above the level of just a research report as the final product and if fieldwork students show a desire for a learning process that is as complete as possible.

In the foregoing, various suggestions have been made for ways in which to carry out the analysis and draw conclusions from the material that is available. By way of a conclusion, we would like to add two practical tips:

■ Wherever possible, try to formulate the conclusions in neutral and verifiable wording, including statements of fact. Avoid expressions like: 'I think' and 'in my opinion' when describing the situation. Phrases that are better used are: 'from the interviews it appears that ...' or 'the documentation reflects ...'. Thus, you can avoid being challenged on these observations because people think they reflect your own opinion. Things are less delicate in the formulation of the proposal for the problem definition and plan of action. After all, they do reflect your own opinion, which may certainly be recognizable.

■ Make sure that individual contributions by interviewees cannot be recognized in the observations and conclusions. In such formulations that are oriented towards people, suggestions of blame and failure may unwittingly creep in, with all the consequences this has for the intended process of aligning all the parties involved.

All the activities that have been described above are the result of an in-depth analysis and use of the knowledge of the organization that has been obtained. All this now has to be worked out and neatly arranged in a presentation that will be given at the feedback session. The next step is dedicated to this session.

List of action points

A summary of the process steps that need to be carried out in the analysis stage is as follows:

1. Use the stacking method
2. Analyse
3. Study the literature
4. Draw conclusions
5. Draw up a proposal for a definite assignment formulation
6. Design a global plan of action
7. Prepare the presentation for the feedback session
8. Complete the relevant pages in the logbook
9. Consult the fieldwork supervisor.

Chapter notes

[1] For processing interview results, see Emans (2004).

[2] Practical instructions for drawing up a good flow chart can be found in the famous Memory Jogger by Brassard and

Ritter (1994: 56) and in the Project Management Memory Jogger by Martin *et al.* (1997).

[3] A similar concept is used by Kubr (2002: 226), who refers to a 'co-operating team'.

[4] The Memory Joggers can also be useful for drawing up a cause–effect diagram or an Ishikawa fishbone analysis.

Exercises for Step 4

7.1   Product innovation project for Coffee-makers Ltd

Marion James – in search of an interesting graduation project – contacted Coffee-makers Ltd. Her timing was perfect because only one day earlier the management team had decided that a product innovation project that was about to be completed needed to be evaluated. In various ways, the project had gone very unsatisfactorily: it had all taken much too long, it had become too expensive and, when the product was finally ready, its chances of commercial success appeared much less favourable than initially expected. In short, an important project for the most part seemed to be a failure. A good evaluation from an outsider was to provide learning points for the company so in the future it would be able to do better in innovation projects. The Human Resources manager was asked to find a suitable fieldwork student. Marion carried out an external orientation and subsequently had an intake meeting with the manager in question, at which her fieldwork supervisor was also present.

They agreed on an initial assignment formulation: to evaluate the course of the 'mini-coffee-maker project'; to make recommendations for improvement of the procedure in the product development process; and to support the implementation of those measures.

It was agreed that Marion would start with some orientational interviews. Reports of a number of interviews subsequently held by Marion are given below.

A selection from the list of points of attention that Marion used in the interviews is as follows:

- Introduction
- The reason for the innovation project

- The involvement of the interviewee in the project
- How does the interviewee look back on the project – what went wrong?
- The reasons that the problems occurred
- Suggestions for improvement.

Interview 1: Managing director, Mr Stewart

The 'mini-coffee-maker project' was started after the managing director had visited a home appliance fair abroad, where he had seen a new type of coffee-maker that worked quickly and had an attractive exterior. The machine could be used in two ways: it could fill a coffeepot or fill cup after cup. The entire machine could easily be built into a kitchen unit. The managing director could not understand why it had never occurred to him to make such a mini-coffee-maker for household use. There had to be a market for it: people who come home tired and like to have a cup of coffee immediately. Normally they would first have to fill the machine with water, put coffee in the filter, plug in the machine and wait until the coffee is ready. With the same quality standards this process should be able to run much more quickly. The machine he had seen could be programmed by means of a number of touch-sensitive keys in such a way that each person could get his or her 'preferred' cup of coffee.

Back at the company, he had asked his product development manager why they had not come up with this idea. He had also told him that, if the company wanted the product to be a commercial success, such a machine would have to be on the market within six months. That was now 18 months ago.

Things immediately went wrong in the management team, where more than six months was lost on discussions about the project. Management was hesitant about the necessary investment, which amounted to €1.25 million, because of the new and advanced technology that would be needed. The production line would have to be changed drastically. And what should they do with their other coffee-makers: would they still be able to sell those once they had switched to the new line? All these objections could not easily be eliminated. The solution was found in co-operation with a large kitchen unit manufacturer.

In the end, the managing director persevered. It had to be now or never! The product development manager was ordered to take on the project and have it completed within seven months, because that was when the kitchen unit manufacturer wanted to launch the machine.

Soon the first problems arose. It was a rather complicated appliance; it was compact, had to have the possibility of ventilation and a steam outlet being built in, involved chip technology, and had to fit in with respect to the design of all sorts of modern kitchens. The project manager who was assigned the project fell ill after one month. A new project manager was assigned. In retrospect, this person did not really have the personality that was needed to bring the people from the various units together within the product development department. He also did not possess any technical know-how on chip technology.

The budget was exceeded by several fold. This was caused by the fact that the computer end of product development had been contracted out to a company that did not know anything about the coffee-maker sector. The company expected that the computer end would be ready and delivered at the agreed time, and that after testing of some models only minor revisions would be necessary before the product could be completed. However, things did not work out as expected. In addition, the kitchen unit manufacturer changed the specifications a number of times.

With an important trade fair imminent, the kitchen unit manufacturer had asked whether the machine could be finished six weeks earlier than planned. The managing director had promised that − 'What else could I do?' This promise had not been checked for feasibility.

The project went wrong on details: planning, quality control, etc.

Regarding the question of suggestions for improvement, the managing director replied that the company staff were not familiar with working in this new way with various partners − supplier and customer − and that the company should learn to do this better.

Interview 2: Project manager, Mr Dirck

General impression
Mr Dirck does not feel 'personally threatened' by this evaluation. He sees it as a good opportunity to bring up learning points, particularly with respect to the external factors he could not control: arrangements that management made with the customer,

arrangements with the supplier, technical difficulties. When he became involved, many things had already been established.

Matters arising from the interview
Mr Dirck was handed over management of the project from a previous project manager who had reported sick due to over-work. Mr Dirck had not received any written notes; the project had been handed over with some verbal instructions. He had to improvise constantly. There had been many problems: changes in specifications by the manufacturer of kitchen units causing budget overruns, technical discussions with the supplier of chip technology, and safety problems (quick heating of water and heat dissipation). The milestones in the project had been determined externally; Dirck himself had not used any milestones or phasing. When the test models had to be made and a production line had to be set up, it was difficult to get the necessary production staff. Dirck felt like a beggar. Despite his complaints, the managing director had not solved this capacity problem. Additional costs caused by the fact that the customer wanted the delivery date to be advanced were booked as incidentals. Internal co-operation with the developers proceeded with great difficulty; it was a 'black box' for Dirck, so contracting out was also not an option. Dirck did not have employees at his disposal that had been released from other tasks; if he needed a planner or controller, he had to try to release capacity from another project.

At present, no product has yet been released. Dirck does not know the extent of the damage to the kitchen unit manufacturer.

Suggestions for improvement
In Dirck's opinion, a change in culture should be brought about: 'technology dominates'. People too easily shout that we can solve everything ourselves. 'Whatever the cost, we will be ready in time'.

Dirck did not know what the competition was doing, or how they solved this type of problem.

Planning should be improved and at times where capacity is needed, it has to be available. The relations with the suppliers were reasonable ('They could not do anything else'), but a better contract should have been made with the customer. 'I don't know who is now paying for the changes that had to be made at the insistence of the kitchen unit manufacturer'.

Dirck is hoping that discipline in the company will improve by means of better project management.

Interview 3: Manager of the technical development department, Mr Farlake

General impression

With little social talk, he wants to step up to the whiteboard immediately (to draw a chart of the organization). In his opinion, the project is important; he thinks the contribution of his own development department is opening up new horizons. A number of his employees were members of the project team. He is immediately prepared to arrange activities. He suggests I have a talk with the managing director of the kitchen unit manufacturer (I must first discuss this with the assignment principal). Farlake has had to solve many problems with respect to throughput times in this project himself. In a way, he felt he was also project manager.

Matters arising from the interview

The mini-coffee-maker project had started rather suddenly. A few months before discussions on this project started, it had been agreed within the management team that a road map for innovation projects would be employed. This meant that instead of spontaneously taking up projects someone happened to like the idea of, they had to look more systematically at future market developments (technology and customers). Then the managing director suggested this idea. 'Taking up something on a whim, that's just what we had agreed we would no longer do'. But still they started the project, because it was very interesting from a technological viewpoint. There was a problem with finding a project manager. The first project manager really had too many projects on hand at the same time. He therefore had to step back. Fortunately, just at that moment someone else became available who had done well in other projects. He then happened to be without a project so he could step right in.

There have been problems with throughput times. The project is taking much too long. This also costs a lot of money. Important causes were that they received the specifications from the kitchen unit manufacturer too late. In addition, these specifications were changed a few times. At a particular time, the project manager could not stand up to the pressure of constantly making alterations. Then their managing director had a meeting with the managing director from the kitchen unit manufacturer. This had solved a lot. It was agreed that if our or their project manager were faced with a problem, it would not be solved quickly, but the managing directors would contact each other by telephone.

Internally there were also problems with respect to fine-tuning of activities. The technological development department designs and develops the technological part of the project, the design department models the exterior. This needs fine-tuning: the exterior must 'fit' the interior and vice versa. The designers form a distinctly separate group, with distinct views on what is or is not possible; they have an artistic streak. Farlake calls them a 'black box'. Initial agreements are made and then you do not know whether they are on schedule or having problems. They keep telling you, 'We'll contact you when we're finished'. In this project, you need to have each other's specifications: the designers must know the requirements from a technological viewpoint and vice versa. Each time the designers were too late in delivering their specifications. There was also trouble with the production side: people who had to staff the production line had not been trained, they did not have any drawings or plans, and new machinery had been installed with which they did not yet have any experience.

Farlake cannot say much about the prognosis of the project. The commercial side of it is unclear.

Suggestions for improvement

Internal decision-making on the start of new projects, the co-operation between the technology and design departments, the deployment of the production department, and the co-operation with customers need to be improved.

Interview 4: Manager of the design department, Mr Jones

General impression

Mr Jones rearranged the date for the interview several times. In the end, the interview took place at 7.30 a.m. Jones works from dawn till dark. The way he talks about 'my people' gives me the impression he is really in charge of the department: he takes all decisions on content and extent of the deployment of the employees in his department. If project manager Dirck has problems with any of the people in this department, he must deal with Jones, who is higher than he is hierarchically.

Matters arising from the interview

The problems in the project lie in the field of quality: the ideas on quality from the development department, the design department and the manufacturer of the kitchen units vary greatly. The way things are now, market expectations are disappointing. Jones has the impression that the manufacturer of kitchen units is starting to have doubts as well. He himself has had doubts from the beginning; he would rather have applied himself to surpassing the new Italian designs. 'Look at what Philips is doing, they are working on creating their own line, which is something we don't do enough.' The discussions in the management team had been very difficult; the excellent market expectations had been the deciding factor.

In Jones's view, they are now paying for the fact that the company has not yet had any real experience with developing a product for customers as large as the kitchen unit manufacturer. 'We did not get a clear picture of the actual relationship: are we co-producers or suppliers? If such a thing is not clear, you will start to doubt the expectations: who pays for interim changes in specifications that are being made? Now we are saying that we'll sort it out later'.

Jones thinks the problem also lies in the capacities of the project manager. The development department handles the selection of project managers too lightly. The first one was, in fact, already overworked when he started. The second one just happened to be available at the time. 'They should not have done that to this man'. He feels that Farlake has drawn the same conclusion now as well and has started to act as project manager.

Jones says that he has had dinner with the person who is responsible for this project on behalf of the kitchen unit manufacturer (assistant manager Moore). He does not want to say much about it, but thinks I should have a talk with this woman.

Suggestions for improvement

Jones thinks the organization should deal with its product development activities in a more professional manner. He thinks there is something to be said for working with a steering committee composed of the decision-makers of the departments involved and maybe also of the customer. In such a committee, decisions can be made. He refers also to suggestions someone from his department made some time ago in this respect. That may not have been the right moment, but it would be important to have another look at that document (document has been requested).

Interview 5: Assistant manager of the kitchen unit manufacturer, Mrs Moore

General impression

This meeting was arranged without a hitch. At first Mr Stewart found it a bit odd that I wanted to visit the customer to talk about the problem, but when I informed him that some of the interviewees found it really important, he gave his consent. Subsequently he phoned the customer himself to arrange the meeting. That went well. I could visit them within one week. Within the firm of Katz, Mrs Moore is responsible for product innovation. She tells me that they do business with suppliers fairly often, but then it concerns existing products: dishwashers, ovens, microwaves, cookers. In those cases, things are much simpler: you just make a programme of requirements, have meetings with a number of possible suppliers and make a contract. Here it concerns something new to them: the product still has to prove itself. Moore remarks that errors have been made on both sides. Communication was not what one could call optimal. At management level, some tough nuts have been cracked; now the air has been cleared again. Moore is extraordinarily interested in my report. She suggests that I also hold a presentation at her company.

Matters arising from the interview

Things were not formalized enough. Principle agreements had been made, which was considered to be enough for such an experiment. More should have been arranged with respect to finances. Looking back, Mrs Moore thinks her company let itself be won over too easily by Stewart's idea, because that was all Stewart had, in fact, an idea; a very attractive one, but it still had to be worked out. Stewart had told them about a product he had seen at some fair, but Moore had not been able to find this product anywhere. However, she still expects the product to become successful commercially. Marketing the mini-coffee-maker has been put on the back-burner, because the development problems first need to be solved.

The discussions with respect to quality have been tough. The product needed to be worked on from different standards. The managing directors have been able to overcome the deadlock.

Moore is inclined to think that Coffee-makers Ltd could copy or purchase more technology than they are doing. The technological solutions they are now trying to find are probably on sale somewhere else already. Developing everything yourself takes a lot of time and money.

She appreciates that they see her as the one who is 'rushing' them, but she thinks that this is her role in this undertaking. After all, the project is taking much longer than originally expected. Soon there will be another fair where she wants to be present with a new product. This new product can still become a success.

Suggestions for improvement

Moore thinks it is not her job to make suggestions for improvements to Coffee-makers Ltd. She will only limit herself to co-operation. That could be better. If there is ever another project like this one, there will have to be a combined project management, a joint project start-up, something like a steering committee, and some clear agreements on how to deal with setbacks. Moore now also looks at the project as a learning process.

Assignments

1   Stack the results of the reports on the interviews that have been described. Use the selection from the list with points of attention the student used (see above).
2   Develop the presentation for the feedback session that will come next.
3   Will it be possible to keep the assignment as formulated at the first meeting with Mr Stewart? If not, make a proposal for a new assignment formulation.
4   What are the main questions Marion must try to find answers to in her in-depth research?
5   Should a platform group be established in this graduation project? If so, who would you like to participate?
6   Will you accept Mrs Moore's suggestion that you should give a presentation to her company? Give reasons for your answer.

Chapter 8

Step 5: Feedback/contracting

The feedback meeting has already been arranged during the intake session and recorded in the diaries of those concerned. All those who have already been interviewed are also invited to this meeting, which will last about 2.5 hours.

The feedback meeting is of vital importance to the success of the consultancy project. This is when those concerned must agree on the definition of the problem, the formulation of the assignment and the plan of action. The success criteria for the project are also reviewed.[1] In other words, this is when the contract is finalized. For this reason, the fieldwork supervisor must also be present.

The targets that must be achieved can be summarized as follows:

- Explaining the information gathered and the insights thus obtained
- Reaching a consensus on the proposed fieldwork assignment
- Obtaining approval for the plan of action being proposed
- Agreeing on the methods to be used in carrying out the assignment.

To illustrate the type of results we have in mind, look at the checklist for Step 5, and see how it can be filled in after the feedback has taken place. Table 8.1 shows a case study involving a seed company whose profit margin has been declining for some time. The student's initial assignment was to investigate the procedural conflicts between the Production and Purchasing departments and to improve these by means of better communication. The orientation stage indicated that the conflicts could be traced back to a fundamental issue in the organization: should

Table 8.1

Example of a completed logbook page for Step 5

Checklist – Step 5: Feedback meeting and contracting	
Questions	**Answers**
1 Do those present agree on the problem definition, the assignment formulation and the proposed approach?	• Problem: declining profit margin • Assignment: advice concerning the decentralization of production and purchasing • Approach: market research, study of competition, goods flow analysis, work groups for implementation (see feedback presentation)
2 How has the assignment changed since the intake and why?	• Original assignment: solve conflict between production/purchasing and sales. Assignment is now more specific, because the conflict is related to the issue of decentralization as a means for improving profit margins
3 What is the intended result of the project?	• That a start has been made on implementing the recommendations (acceptable to all those concerned) for decentralization of production and purchasing, with the aim of achieving a higher turnover
4 What are the (general) requirements that the solution must satisfy?	• It must be possible to implement the proposals within six months. The solution must be acceptable: no compulsory redundancies, but retraining of personnel where necessary is admissible
5 What indications are there that the project is important to the company?	• The director stated at a meeting with personnel that this project is the main item on his agenda for the coming year
6 Are the principal and the company management motivated to actually implement the solution?	• See answer to question 5
7 What further information is necessary for drawing up a working schedule?	• Market facts and logistic information
8 Who are the members of the platform group?	• Director, purchasing manager, production manager, sales manager
9 What arrangements have been agreed for the work to be done?	• Company will provide the remaining information within two weeks • Within three weeks, I will present the detailed work plan at the management team meeting
10 Remarks	

Production and Purchasing be managed centrally or would it be more profitable to create internal customer–supplier relationships between Sales, Production and Purchasing? After a discussion with those concerned, the assignment was modified. A consensus was also reached on the approach the student would follow and the information that would be necessary, and how quickly the information should be available. Since a fundamental problem for the company was involved, it was decided that four members of the management team would be included in the platform group.

It is clear that results of this type can only be achieved if the feedback session is properly prepared. We will discuss a number of organizational measures for promoting the success of the meeting.

Organization of the feedback session

Before the feedback session, check that:

1   Sufficient time (1.5–2.5 hours) has been reserved for the meeting
2   All the interviewees invited will be present on time
3   Nobody will be present who has not been interviewed.

If these three requirements are not met to a considerable extent, it is better to plan a new meeting in consultation with the principal and fieldwork supervisor, rather than run the risk of a contract with insufficient support. A professional consultant would certainly request a new appointment.

The second and third points may require some explanation. To gain total acceptance of the problem definition and to develop support for the streamlined assignment and the overall plan of action, as many of those interviewed as possible must be present. If some are missing, you will have to update them later on and obtain their backing for your proposals. This means extra work, and you will miss out on the open discussion that is sometimes necessary. So insist on people's presence as much as you can by ensuring that the secretaries book the meeting in their diaries in good time (directly after the intake session).

But why exclude people who have not been interviewed, as stated in point 3? This is because they have not contributed to the vision that is being presented, and may be unreasonably unco-operative about this. All those directly concerned with the consultancy process should participate in the interview programme and must therefore also attend the feedback meeting. Others who are less directly concerned will be informed indirectly at a later stage – for example, by means of a concise report. On several occasions, we have witnessed hostile discussions caused by outsiders, and have had to intervene firmly as fieldwork supervisors to keep the meeting headed in the right direction. It can happen that a student realizes at the last minute that someone directly involved appears to have been 'forgotten' in the interviews. The best remedy in this case is to interview the person as soon as possible, incorporate his or her views into the presentation and invite him or her to the feedback meeting.

Once the meeting has been properly organized, pay attention to the following points:

■ Try to arrange for the chairman of the meeting (preferably the managing director) to introduce you and stress the importance of the meeting.

■ Start with a draft agenda for the meeting and check that everybody agrees with this. An example of a good agenda is given below.

Example 8.1: Agenda for the meeting on ... on the subject of the fieldwork assignment

15.00	1	Opening	(managing director)
15.10	2	Presentation of interview findings	(student)
15.40	3	Discussion	(all present)
16.00	4	Presentation of assignment definition and general plan of action	(student)
16.30	5	Discussion and decision	(all present)
17.00	6	Proposal for communication plan	(company coach)
17.15	7	Follow-up agreements	(all present)
17.30	8	Questions and conclusion	(managing director)

In the agenda, the discussion on the findings and the discussion on the assignment definition and plan of action are kept separate. The reason for this is the different objectives of the two activities. When discussing the findings, the aim is to confirm that those concerned recognize the picture described and that the student has properly understood the situation. When discussing the assignment definition and plan of action, the aim is for everyone concerned to accept the proposals and be prepared to co-operate with them. It is important to explicitly mention these differing objectives at the beginning of the meeting when going through the agenda, so that the issues do not overlap too much during the discussions.

- ■ Provide professional transparencies and check in advance that there is a working overhead projector or beamer (with screen and pointer) available in the meeting room.
- ■ Bring a printed copy of the transparencies/slides for each person present, but do not distribute these until after the presentation of the subject in question. This is to avoid losing people's attention because they are looking through their copies during the presentation. After the presentation, the attendees should be given the opportunity to look through their handouts, and any remaining discussion points can be covered.
- ■ At the end, undertake to provide all those present with a brief report on the presentation and the discussion to complete the contracting procedure. This means that notes must be taken during the discussions.
- ■ Agree on what further decisions must be taken concerning the plan of action presented. In general, the go-ahead for the student to continue the work will be given during the meeting. In large organizations, it is often necessary for other decision-makers to be consulted. Emphasizing the need for fast decision-making can prevent an irritating delay.

Unexpected developments may arise during the meeting; it is possible that some findings may not be understood. The best reaction to this is to ask questions during the discussion in order to incorporate changes, additions or more detail. This can generally be achieved with the assistance of the company coach and the fieldwork supervisor.

It may become clear that different visions exist concerning the contents of the proposed assignment. In this case, it is best to discuss them straight away. The chairman must lead this discussion as, strictly speaking, the company is responsible for a uniform interpretation of the assignment.

Contents of the feedback presentation

The student does not always realize that, at this stage, he or she is the only person engaged in the investigation. This means the presentation must be constructed in such a way that everyone can pick up the thread easily. Do not rush straight to the point, as this means the listeners will not become familiar enough with the subject to discuss it satisfactorily. Bearing this in mind, it is wise to start the presentation with the *original problem definition* from the first meeting. After that, explain the *research work* carried out to obtain a deeper insight. This should include the list of those interviewed, the documentation reviewed and the specific points focused on during those orientational activities. The themes from the interview list discussed in Steps 3 and 4 must also be mentioned.

This manner of presentation helps ensure that everybody is on the right track. The summary of the activities carried out not only serves a 'warming up' function, but also acts as an introduction to the working methods. Occasionally, criticisms are made about documentation that was not reviewed or people who were not interviewed. It is important that such comments should be heard, because it is still possible at this stage to correct such shortcomings after the meeting. This feedback session offers the opportunity to discover and deal with any matters that were not covered during the orientational interviews for any reason.

The next step in the presentation is to display the business processes that are relevant to the assignment, such as the production flow chart and the distribution of tasks and responsibilities. At first sight, this item may appear superfluous in a presentation of this nature, as one can assume that those who are present on the company's behalf will know how the processes are structured. But the importance is not in its informative value, but in the confidence it can generate: those present will see that the student understands how the company operates. If there are any gaps in understanding, these will now be brought to light so that they can be corrected quickly.

After that, attention should be paid to the *findings* from the orientation programme. The respondents' vision of the details of the problem is the prime consideration here. If views on this differ, the feedback session is the ideal opportunity to identify this and talk about it.

It is important to pay attention to differences in views during the discussion. Managers often attribute little importance to differences of opinion. Consultants know that part of their success depends on appreciating the fundamental aims and expectations of the group. Disagreements frequently offer an excellent opportunity to obtain a better idea of what is important for the company and what priorities the managers have. Unfortunately, many people have a tendency to shy away from conflict rather than to learn from it. Discussion should be possible, with assistance from the fieldwork supervisor if necessary.

One of us experienced a good example of a situation of this type at a steel company. The assignment was to make deliveries match up better with customers' expectations. In his plan of action, the student had correctly included the intention of interviewing a representative number of customers. The sales manager protested against this, as he was afraid of losing customers because of a clumsy approach. The discussion – which had been anticipated by the student and discussed with his fieldwork supervisor – was fierce, as others were strongly in favour of the student's approach. After some heated debate, the fieldwork supervisor proposed that the student should draw up the list of questions in consultation with Sales, that Sales should help select the customers and that the student should conduct the interviews in the presence of a salesman. This proposal gave the sales manager sufficient confidence that he would be in control of the risks, and the plan was then approved.

After the presentation of the findings, an extensive discussion is appropriate. The following questions should be focused on: Does everybody recognize the picture painted? Does the diagnosis match up with everybody's expectations? Once this discussion has been concluded satisfactorily, we can move on to the presentation of the assignment and the *plan of action*, as a logical follow-on from the agreed problem definition. The plan of action contains concrete details of the agreed assignment definition. The activities are specified and placed in a logical order. The reason for presenting this general work plan is to make it clear that the assignment is feasible and the objective can be achieved.

We have previously pointed out how important it is that the investigation is based on sound management consultancy principles. However, the feedback presentation is neither the time nor place to state these principles in detail. It is only necessary for the student to specify the main activities, which are partly governed by these theoretical considerations. If requested in the discussion, a brief explanation can be given of what professional knowledge will be used to carry out the assignment. This is down to the expertise of the individual student.

In the plan of action, the updated assignment definition must be a prime consideration.[2] This states in concise terms what the client can expect at the end of the project. The more the project is defined in measurable terms, the easier it will be to establish afterwards whether the promised results have been achieved. A contributing factor is whether the student focuses the contract on the execution of an investigation or the achievement of an observable organizational improvement – for example, reducing production losses by 20 per cent.

In organizational consultancy work we call the first situation (an investigation) an *activity contract* and the second (an organizational change to be implemented) a *results contract*. The classic activity contract is generally formulated in terms such as 'research into...', 'advice concerning...' or sometimes 'consultancy during the introduction of...'. A contract of this type emphasizes that the student will help to make matters clearer and more transparent, and will make proposals that will require further decisions, but that the responsibility for further action rests with the client. The consultant is responsible for the quality of the advice, not for the implementation. But there is currently a move towards the results contract in preference to the classic activity contract. More and more clients are objecting to the lack of involvement on the part of consultants. They believe that the quality of advice will be better if the consultant also takes responsibility for achieving the intended end result. More and more consultancies are responding to this wish from their clients and they sometimes even go so far as to make their fee partly dependent on the results of their work. Naturally, this is only possible in consultancy areas where the results of the work can easily be measured. Examples of these are:

■ Filling a job vacancy
■ Finding a merger partner
■ Reducing the level of absence due to illness
■ Increasing the productivity of factories
■ Improving logistic performance.

This move towards the results contract adds weight to our emphasis on learning how to implement during fieldwork projects.[3]

It is clear that the consultant who commits to actually achieving improvements in organizational processes will think more carefully about the feasibility of the proposals than would otherwise be the case. Moreover, more attention will be paid to the change-directed aspect of implementing the assignment. Since quality and acceptance are the key factors here, we tend to encourage students to work with result-oriented contracts as much as possible. Even students must learn to share responsibility in the sense that they practise establishing a direct link between the contribution made by their own fieldwork project and the company results. After all, in their future working environment, this will also play a role, in fact even more so. Obviously, you should not promise more than you think you can deliver. This approach fits in with our basic principle that an advisory report should never be an objective in itself.

A fieldwork project will seldom lead to a large-scale improvement in the company results, but students can consciously keep these in mind during their work. There are examples of students who managed to achieve substantial savings within companies by improving ways of working or by introducing new methods and systems.

You will have the potential to achieve this kind of success in your work if, during the feedback session, you try to obtain acceptance of an assignment definition along the following lines:

■ Give advice on how the turnover of product x can be increased by 10 per cent per year
■ Provide support in one of the sales offices during the implementation of this advice.

This sounds very different from 'investigate the possibilities for increasing turnover'. This formulation shows that reducing the scope – for example, substituting one sales office for the entire organization – is often the key to being able to participate in the implementation phase even in the limited fieldwork period. If the assignment definition is streamlined in this way during the feedback session, a corresponding plan of action is required. The company cannot say yes to an assignment without understanding the associated efforts and costs.

As already indicated, a plan of action is a summary of the work that the student considers necessary in order to produce the intended recommendations. This plan should state who will carry out this work. Although a fieldwork project is something that you carry out independently as a student, it does not mean you have to do everything yourself. It is sensible to request assistance from others within the company, sometimes because they have the necessary expertise, but also to increase their involvement in producing the final recommendation. A few examples of activities that can be 'delegated' are:

- Collecting data such as stock levels, order sizes, complaints from customers, absenteeism figures, processing times in the factory
- Market research by the sales staff, or possibly outsourced (fully or in part) to an external market research agency
- Brainstorming sessions led by the student
- Research by work groups that carry out an in-depth analysis of a specific aspect – for example, the operation of the quality control system.

Students who include a number of activities to be delegated in their plan of action will generally have to take responsibility for organizing and supervising the execution of these activities. After all, the structure, content and quality of the work must fit in with the defined investigation.

Another important item in the presentation is the *communication plan*. To make sure the advisory process is firmly embedded in the organization, regular consultation with the parties concerned is necessary. Aspects that should be covered are:

- Role of the company coach(es)
- Composition and role of the steering group
- Periodic (e.g. monthly) interim reports, to be discussed by the management team
- Consultations with the people or work groups involved in carrying out the work.

Making clear agreements on these points helps ensure that the investigation remains at the centre of interest and that a solid foundation is laid for the acceptance and implementation of the recommendations.

Sometimes a number of support facilities need to be arranged during the feedback session. This generally means things like easily accessible working space with a telephone, computer, secretarial assistance and possibly an agreed budget for work to be outsourced (e.g. market research).

The feedback session is finally closed by the chairman with a summary of the main conclusions, and the student's promise to send everybody (within a week if possible) a summary of the presentation, the discussion, the decisions taken and the agreements made. It is best to add a separate plan of action to this, which incorporates the latest changes.

Figure 8.1 is an example of a feedback presentation for the previously mentioned project within a seed company. Naturally, it is advisable to pay attention to the presentation technique. Up to now, we have focused primarily on the agenda of the feedback session – what needs to be covered? Within organizational consultancy work, it is not just the contents of a presentation that are important, but also the form in which it is given. A professional advisor repeatedly asks the question: How can I deliver my message in such a way that it will be understood and acted upon? Students, too, should ask themselves in advance: What can I do to make the feedback session as effective as possible? Several aspects have already been dealt with: preparing an agenda for the meeting, an agenda for the presentation, result-oriented assignment definition, preliminary consultation with the chairman/principal and the fieldwork supervisor (making sure that the latter is also present at the feedback session) and checking that necessary facilities will be available.

There are good publications on preparing and giving professional presentations, and attention is paid to presentation techniques during most courses. We will therefore limit ourselves here to mentioning the following rules of thumb.[4]

Know your audience

Gear the presentation to your audience. This requires thought when giving examples (are they clear and illustrative for everyone?) and if you plan to relate any anecdotes (will everybody appreciate this?). Follow the basic rule that nobody will be attending the feedback session whom you have not already interviewed. If someone who is not familiar with the project and has not been interviewed still wishes to attend, then it is advisable to talk to that person beforehand. During this meeting, you can introduce yourself and inform the other person about the reasons for the project and its objectives, and about the approach that has been followed up to that point.

	Agenda slides	Contents of presentation

Project
Profit improvement
Seed company
 	
Feedback presentation
 	
Karin de Bondt 16-5-2004
	1. Opening
	2. Report on orientation phase a/h
	3. Discussion i
	4. Proposed assignment and
	   approach j/k/l
	5. Discussion and decision
	6. Communication plan m
	7. Follow-up agreements n
	8. Any questions and closure
		• Report on orientation phase a/h
		• Points for discussion i
		• Proposed assignment and
		   approach j/k/l
		• Proposal for communication plan m
		• Follow-up agreements n

Report on orientation phase a	**Initial statement of problem** b	**Sources of information** c

Sector developments
• Seed trade has become global
   business
• Very large players due to mergers
• Necessity of major investments in
   research (genetic modification)
   and quality control
	• Traditional company
	• Expansion to international scale
	• Global competition
	• Turnover stabilization
	• Shrinking profit due to increasing costs
	• Assignment: advice on profit
	   improvement
		• Interviews with:
		- Director Mr Jones
		- Purchasing Manager Mr Zadoli
		- Production Manager Ms. Black
		- Branch Managers: USA Mr Johnson,
		   UK Mr Jones
		- Controller Mr Dillen
		- Works Council chair Ms. Roorda

Sources of information (continued) d	**Findings** g	**Findings (continued)** h

• Documentation study
• Brochures
• Strategy plan: Towards profit
• Minutes of Board meetings
• Branch investigation report
• Decentralization advisory report
	• Little insight into market
	• Prognosis: losses next year
	• General vision: something must be
	   done before it is too late
	• Varying visions on how to improve:
	- Production/Purchasing vision:
	   upscaling via merger, improving
	   logistics, keep Purchasing and
	   Production centrally managed
		• Sales vision: increasing autonomy per
		   country, more local purchasing, only
		   purchasing for specials and support
		   for countries managed centrally
		• Competitors are more decentralized
		   and have better logistics
		• Need for independent vision in order
		   to increase profit

Points for discussion i	**Proposed assignment and approach** j	**Proposed plan of action** k

• Recognizable picture?
• Vision of causes?
• How can differences in vision
   be solved?
• Support for contribution from student?
	• Advice for increasing profit by >10%
	• Partly based on desirable balance
	   between central and non-central
	   activities
	• Initiation of implementation
		• Market research by external agency
		• Process analysis of logistic flows
		   and identification of improvements by
		   work group led by Karin
		• Structure study led by Karin making
		   use of:
		- interviews
		- brainstorming sessions

Proposed plan of action l	**Proposed communication plan** m	**Further agreements on execution** n

• Platform group:
- Director
- Purchasing Manager
- Production Manager
- two (national) sales managers
• Pilot project for implementing the new
   approach in two national organizations
	• Weekly meeting of platform group
	• Monthly presentation for management
	   team
	• Further definition of project
	   organization
	• Own feature in personnel publication
	   for progress reports
	• Monthly updates for Works Council
		• Decision on proposal in management
		   team meeting Mon 6 June
		• Report to be drawn up by Karin on the
		   basis of slides and discussion (Before
		   MT on Monday)
		• Agency selection for market research
		   (Karin + Director)
		• Detailed work plan (Karin)

Figure 8.1

Model feedback presentation.

Flow diagram of seed purchasing, propagation, sales   e

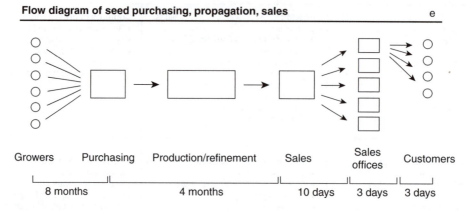

Growers	Purchasing	Production/refinement	Sales	Sales offices	Customers

8 months   4 months   10 days   3 days   3 days

Delivery and production times

Organization diagram   f

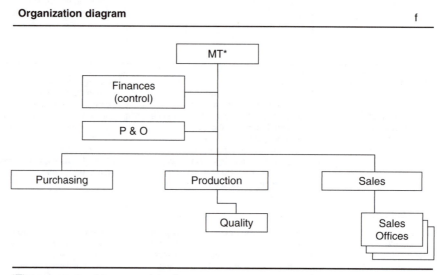

*The management team consists of:
- Managing Director
- Purchasing Director
- Production Director
- Sales Director

Figure 8.1
contd.

Without a preliminary meeting, there is a strong chance that this person will not consider himself bound by the more or less explicit agreements that have already been made during the intake meeting and during the explanatory part of the interviews.

Clear and concrete message

The audience must be able to follow the message without difficulty. The essence of the presentation must be recognizable: the proposals for the definition of the problem and assignment and for the approach to be followed. This essence must be backed by clear arguments. To keep the main thread of the presentation visible, it is a good idea to indicate when the focus shifts from one item to the next, and to summarize at intervals what has already been said.

Keep an eye on the time

Make sure that the meeting does not take longer than the time agreed. Contribute to this yourself by limiting your speaking time to a maximum of half an hour. Check your watch inconspicuously at intervals. It should be possible to convey the main points in half an hour. Remember that you will have the chance of explaining details during the discussion. On the other hand, you should certainly not have said all you have to say in five minutes. Rather timid students sometimes want to get through their presentation as quickly as possible and have a tendency to rattle off an extremely brief monologue at top speed. This does not promote credibility and authority, especially as it then appears that you have not studied the issue in much depth. Help from the fieldwork supervisor and trial presentations in a familiar environment can help you avoid this pitfall.

We are assuming that all interview participants will attend the entire meeting. Unfortunately, people with full diaries do sometimes leave early. Arrange to inform them personally about any further agreements made.

Use of audio and visual equipment

We have already indicated that the feedback presentation should be supported by clear transparencies or slides that everybody can see via an overhead projector or beamer. It is sometimes a good idea to liven up the presentation – for example, with a short video film or other illustrative material. The main rule here is that the material should augment all or part of the subject matter – for example, a short video about a business process that not every-body is familiar with. This should not last longer than five minutes.

List of action points

At the end of this chapter on how the activities are discussed dur-ing this feedback step, we reiterate the process steps that should be carried out during this phase of the consultancy process:

1 Organize the session
2 Hold the presentation
3 Ensure that a consensus exists on the analysis and the proposal
4 Make agreements for carrying out the work
5 Draw up and distribute a report
6 Fill in the checklist
7 Consult the fieldwork supervisor.

Chapter notes

[1] Block (1999: Chapter 5) describes in detail how a 'contract session' can be prepared and held.

[2] See also Greiner and Metzger (1983: 257): re-evaluating the proposal.

[3] For a more detailed description of the result-directed consul-tancy style, see Hale (1998).

[4] See Mandel (2000) and Emden and Becker (2004).

Exercises for Step 5

8.1 Fieldwork project at Shoemakers Ltd

Jane Jackson is carrying out her fieldwork project at Shoemakers Ltd, a medium-sized manufacturer of men's shoes. She has been given the assignment of reorganizing the goods flow management system in such a way that the stock levels are drastically lowered.

After a series of bad seasons, the shoe shop chains in Europe that Shoemakers Ltd supplies with its products are becoming increasingly unwilling to bear the risk of keeping stocks. The result is that the manufacturer must maintain larger stocks in order to deliver the many repeat orders on time.

Jane has reached the stage in her fieldwork, working in accordance with the TSP model, where she is ready for the feedback session. Her presentation is prepared. She contacts the managing director, who is also her company coach, to set a date for the feedback session. To her dismay, this cannot be held for three weeks because several of the people interviewed will be abroad until then for an important trade fair. But the time eventually comes. However, an hour before the start of the meeting, she discovers that three of the seven people invited left again for Italy the previous evening to deal with a claim for compensation from a large chain of stores. The director reassures her by saying that each of those concerned has arranged for a deputy to attend. Although these deputies have not been interviewed, the director does not anticipate any complications.

At the start of her presentation, she hands out copies of her transparencies at the insistence of one of the deputies. She cannot prevent those present from spending more time leafing through the pages than listening during her talk.

After presenting the findings from the orientational interviews, she opens the discussion on the results, and it then transpires that two of the three deputies are unable to identify with her findings and make cutting remarks about them. Another begins to make comments about the plan of action, which has not yet been presented, because there is no agenda indicating that this will be covered later.

The director/chairman maintains a somewhat passive attitude during the fairly chaotic discussion. The result is that the meeting time of an hour and a half, which was already on the short side, is over before a conclusion has been reached that satisfies Jane. It is decided that the discussion will be continued at a subsequent meeting to be held two weeks later. Hopefully, the absent interviewees will then be present.

1   What points for improvement can you identify in Jane's approach to this feedback session?
2   How could she have influenced the way the chairman acted?
3   How could she circumvent a request to distribute the sheets beforehand?

8.2 Differences in insight

How would you react if the feedback presentation brought to light a fundamental difference of opinion about the assignment and plan of action?

8.3 Measurable terms

Give an example of a fieldwork assignment defined in non-result-oriented terms. Then reformulate this assignment in measurable terms.

Chapter 9

Step 6: Work planning and organization

During the feedback in Step 5, the student presented a high-level action plan. In this plan, the outline of the total project becomes visible. The intended end results are stated, along with the route that will be followed to achieve them. The action plan is built on two foundations: the results of the orientation in the company (interviews and documents) and the results of the discipline-based theoretical study.

This high-level action plan must be developed further by detailing sub-tasks to be carried out at the correct time in order that the project as a whole can be completed successfully. This chapter deals with the process of specifying in detail the research activities that will be carried out in Step 7. Later on – in Step 8 – we will cover the activities necessary for implementing the chosen solution.

Before we address the main theme of this chapter – drawing up a working plan for the in-depth research – we will look briefly at an aspect of methodology that is important for the execution of Steps 6, 7 and 8.

Justification mode

In the methodology literature, a distinction is regularly made between two cycles: the empirical or theoretical cycle and the regulative or practical cycle. The theoretical cycle is followed in research where an explanation for a phenomenon is sought (why does this situation exist?), and the practical cycle in research where an intervention or change is prepared and carried out (what can I do about this?). If a department of a company has a conspicuously high level of absence due to illness, the problem can be approached using both cycles. An investigative structure approached on the basis of the theoretical cycle would mean that the student investigates why the personnel in department A are off sick so much more often than the personnel of the other departments. An assignment definition based on the practical cycle would mean that the student must develop and help implement measures to reduce the observed level of sickness absenteeism in department A. The first assignment yields an answer to the question: Why is the absence due to illness so high in department A? The second assignment results in a reduction of absence due to illness in department A. Either project can be useful.

Earlier in this book, we made it clear that we are in favour of assignments of the practical type. By far the majority of students will be working in practical situations after graduating. The assignments will then be of the practical type: think up an approach for solving this or that problem. So it seems logical to 'practise' with an assignment of this type during your fieldwork.

The reason for mentioning both types of cycle here is to prevent a misunderstanding. The difference between the two cycles is often exaggerated. The point we wish to make is that, in both cases, a 'model' is necessary as justification. This 'model' implies a certain reasoning process about the phenomenon being examined. This reasoning process must be carried out explicitly, which demands special attention in Steps 6, 7 and 8 of the TSP.

A student working on the basis of the theoretical cycle in the sickness absenteeism assignment described will search the literature for possible explanations for differences in sickness absenteeism between and within companies. Examples of findings are that men are off sick for longer than women, women are off sick for shorter periods but more often, older employees are ill more often than younger ones, personnel who carry out physically taxing work are sick more often and for longer than those who carry out lighter physical work, people who enjoy their work are ill less frequently than those who feel they are under pressure, problems at home can cause sickness absenteeism, sickness absenteeism is higher in large departments than in small ones, etc. The student will select several possible explanations that fit in best with what he or she already knows about the company. By comparing what has been found in the literature with the actual organization in which the problem exists, the student can come up with creative research ideas. A research model is drawn up on the basis of these ideas. After that, the study is set in motion to decide which of the possible explanations for the high level of sickness absenteeism is the best one.

A student who starts out using the practical mode will primarily search the literature for options to actually reduce sickness absenteeism. For example, he or she may discover that the following actions have the desired effect: making it compulsory to report sick to one's supervisor; making home visits as quickly as possible; subtracting a number of days of sickness from the annual leave allowance. The student will make a choice from various options for intervention. On the basis of this investigation, the student can draw up his/her own creative model as the starting point for developing measures to be taken in the department concerned.

Both approaches are based on their own reasoning process. This is what we have in mind with the concept of 'justification mode'.

The student must have a model that provides arguments for why any particular intervention will lead to lower sickness absenteeism in the specific context of the company concerned.

We will now continue with the kernel of Step 6: the work planning and project organization.

Work planning and project organization

To ensure that all the lower-level tasks are started in good time and that the whole project is completed on time, a detailed action plan is necessary. With this in mind, careful consideration must be given to the work to be carried out, the time to be spent on it and the time constraints, task distribution, dependencies, feedback milestones, etc.

It is not really in a consultant's nature to work in this detailed and plan-based manner when managing a project. Professionals prefer to play things by ear as events unfold. They like to remain flexible so that they can alter their approach as new developments arise. Their experience has enabled them to develop a certain instinct that allows them to keep the project on track. Moreover, they have learned to estimate the time needed for particular activities and can avoid promising deadlines that are too tight, unless the customer insists.

This way of working becomes more difficult as more people are involved in the project. If a multinational organization hires a large consultancy to examine their global distribution and a team of ten consultants is appointed in order to reduce the time needed for the project, then detailed project planning is indispensable. With assignments like this, tight deadlines for the final report are generally specified in the contract. In such cases little can be left to chance.

Students, too, must take steps to limit the uncertainties in their project. Too many fieldwork assignments achieve less than was promised and too many students find themselves short of time. The reason is generally that they underestimate the scale of the work and the time needed to carry it out, and that they do not make suitable allowance for the dependence on work done by others.

Case 9.1 describes a number of problems in planning the work.

Case 9.1

A national wholesaler in white goods (washing machines, dryers, dishwashers, refrigerators, etc.) decided to reduce its distribution network and instructed a student to provide advice on how to implement this. He had five months to carry out this final fieldwork project. The student decided to start by holding about 20 interviews with sales personnel from the various branches. Because of the full diaries of those concerned, he had considerable difficulty making appointments. The interviews ended up taking about a month and a half. In addition, he promised each respondent an interview report, which he intended to use for further research after receiving their approval. The response time to his interview reports was so long that it was a month after the final interviews before he had received all the replies.

It was clear to him after the interviews that he needed much more market information, particularly on the buying behaviour of the customers and on the sales approaches used by competitors. The management agreed that he could select and commission an external market research agency for this. The selection took two weeks, and the assignment itself one month.

He then planned an interim report to the management team. Because several managers had commitments at a national trade fair where the firm was exhibiting, it was three weeks before he was able to attend a management team meeting.

Meanwhile, his fieldwork supervisor began to press him for a final report, because the fieldwork period was drawing to an end. The student had little choice but to collect together the summary of the interviews and the market research and submit this to the management team with a brief introduction.

To make sure that a fieldwork project has substantial added value for both the company and for the educational institution, the planning of the project is very important.[1] We will discuss a number of planning activities. The checklist (Table 9.1) gives an example of the answers that must be provided based on careful preparation of the in-depth study. The example is taken from a fieldwork project at a brick factory. The assignment consisted of advising the management on a decision in the near future whether or not the company should comply with the local authority's increasingly urgent request to move from the centre of a village to a site on an industrial estate.

A steering group and three work groups have been set up, each of which will carry out separate tasks: customer survey, quality analysis and competition study. All these activities must be carried out in order to obtain the fullest possible picture of the company's future prospects, so that the specifications for the new building work can be geared to this. Since a working method with a steering group and three work groups demands a considerable amount of harmonization, regular reports and consultation sessions have been arranged. The student will perform a double role: supervisor of the work groups, and the expert setting up and carrying out the survey of potential customers.

We will look in more detail at some of the aspects covered in this checklist.

Data collection methods

To set up the working plan and project organization, it is necessary to decide which data collection methods will be used. Possibilities are: participation, interviews, observations, analysis of documents, and measurements. For a description of these methods, see the next chapter, which covers Step 7, in-depth research.

Table 9.1

Example of a completed logbook page for Step 6

Checklist – Step 6: Work planning and project organization	
Questions	**Answers**
1　What information does the literature review provide to assist in the investigation: 　　a　Applicable theories or theoretical concepts? 　　b　Key variables?	• A number of journal articles and books under the keywords: product innovation, workspace design, environmental requirements for establishment or relocation, effects of relocation and modernization on sales prospects. • Key issues: good internal decision-making, risks in starting up new systems, taking advantage of opportunities for promoting new image
2　What data collection methods will need to be used?	• Survey of customers, in-depth interviews with salesmen, request production department to provide process descriptions, interview with secretary of branch association, analysis of information in trade journals
3　What is the planned schedule?	• Start of work groups: 1 September • First report: 1 November • Final report: 15 December
4　Have project groups been formed? If so, what tasks have been assigned?	• Work groups: 　– Customer survey: external service manager + student 　– Quality analysis: production manager, quality control manager + student 　– Competition study: marketing manager and external service manager
5　What role(s) have you chosen?	• Partly supervisory (structure, monitoring, work groups, support during execution), partly expert (carrying out survey of potential customers)
6　What has been agreed about meetings and reports?	• Monthly progress report to steering group • Work groups updated during Friday afternoon meetings
7　How has the organization of the in-depth investigation been recorded? 8　Remarks	• In the feedback session report

Choosing suitable methods

There are many methods available for obtaining the required research data, and we are only able to give a cursory outline of these. For each individual assignment, it is necessary to explore the possibilities thoroughly. Not every method is suitable for every situation. It is the student's task to make the correct choice. In professional consultancy situations, efficiency plays a primary role. For example, interviews are time-consuming and therefore expensive, but they yield detailed information and create a sense of involvement. A written survey of a large group is a relatively cheap method, but is also very superficial. To compensate for the disadvantages of individual methods, combinations can be used. A written survey of a large group of respondents could be supplemented by a limited number of interviews in order to understand the background behind any unexpected survey results.

For students – who only have a limited fieldwork period available – it is important to choose methods that are easy to plan and only require a limited time to carry out.

Intended result of fieldwork project

It is only possible to draw up a working plan once the desired end results of the project have been specified.[2] This has doubtless been discussed during the feedback meeting. The principal wants to know what will have been achieved at the end of the project. When discussing the previous steps, we have already expressed our preference for a results contract. The feedback meeting report describes the intended end product of the activities ('deliverables' is the term often used in professional circles). The planning of the work shows how the agreed target will be achieved.

Work planning

Once the end result of the fieldwork project is specified, a detailed plan can be drawn up. A work plan is an absolute prerequisite for completing the contracted assignment in the time available. Running out of time in a fieldwork project has proved to be one of the greatest risks for devaluing the work done.

The planning must satisfy the requirement that it has value as a working document. This is achieved firstly by providing an overall project plan using a monthly time scale to give a long-term, high-level view, and secondly by providing a detailed activity plan for the coming weeks. The recommended times given for the various phases of the TSP can act as a guideline for planning the project. We indicate below the lines along which the desired plans can be drawn up:

- Specify the main activities needed to carry out the field-work project. A number of approaches for identifying the main activities have already been described in Step 4 (analysis).
- Split the main activities into sub-tasks. At the same time it is useful to think about who will perform the tasks, so that the amount of time required for each can be estimated in consultation with those concerned.
- Estimate the working time and the elapsed time needed for each task and produce totals for each main activity.
- Specify the time period during which each task will be carried out.

A detailed example is given in Table 9.2. The schedule also includes the option to record the actual times taken, which can be used for monitoring progress.

Making regular reports on planning and progress to the principal and the fieldwork supervisor will help you to improve your own working discipline. It also means that any risk of delay will be identified in good time so that it will be possible to discuss ways to make up any lost time. In our experience, fieldwork projects that are properly planned and where timely action is taken to keep on course produce the best results. Consulting a book about network planning is a good investment in this context.[3]

Work groups and choice of advisory roles

Consultancy projects with a defined time scale, such as fieldwork projects, can be made more comprehensive if more people contribute. Students often fail to make enough use of this. They think they must do everything themselves, otherwise they are not providing enough evidence of their capabilities. This is a misunderstanding. This attitude can also be encouraged by supervisors

Table 9.2
Work planning

Main activity	Tasks	To be carried out by:	Work time Plan/days	Work time Actual	Throughput time Plan/days	Throughput time Actual	Time period Plan/week	Time period Actual
1 Client survey	Select customers	External services manager	1		2		35	
	Draw up questionnaire	Student	2		2		36	
	Trial survey	Student	2		5		37	
	Distribution/replies	External services manager	1		20		38–42	
	Processing replies	Student	3		5		42	
			9					
2 Study of own product quality	Analysis of production statements for 2 years	Student	3		5		38	
	Quality review	Independent research agency	?		?		38–?	
3 Analysis of complaints								
4 Product comparison								

Company: Technocon   Project: Increasing turnover   Student: Steven Lane who focus too much on evaluating what students have actually done themselves.

The fieldwork project will be a better reflection of the professional situation that will be encountered later on if the student makes as much use as possible of the potential offered by the company personnel. Luckily, many courses now expressly ask the fieldwork supervisor and company coach whether the student has shown sufficient independence during the project and made enough use of the company's resources.

There are advantages and disadvantages to the two alternatives: 'working on your own' and 'working with others'. Figure 9.1 shows a number of points for consideration.[4] We will illustrate the choice that students face with an example.

Suppose the fieldwork assignment is to develop a strategic plan. If the role of *solo player* is chosen, the work plan could be:

- Interviews with the people concerned
- Study of the market and the competitors
- Analysis of the company's weak and strong points
- Drawing up a strategic plan report
- Submitting the report to the management team.

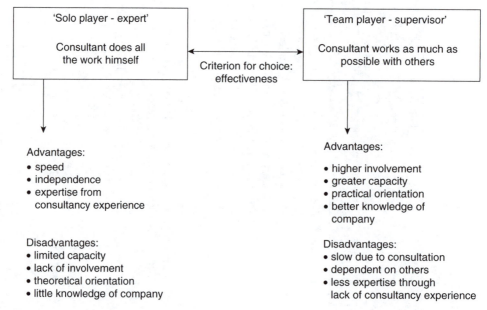

Figure 9.1
Choosing the most effective advisory role.

The role of *team player* may result in the following programme:

- The project group 'Strategy 2010' is set up, consisting of the six management team members. The project group appoints a 'Market' work group and a SWOT work group.
- The Market work group (student and two management team members) carries out studies of the market and the competitors, and presents this to the project group.
- The SWOT work group (student and two management team members) carries out the analysis of strengths and weaknesses (SWOT = Strengths, Weaknesses, Opportunities, Threats).
- The project group holds a two-day workshop to develop a strategic plan based on the analyses presented. The director is chairman; the student is responsible for all the organization and takes responsibility for drawing up a report.
- The workshop results are presented by the director and/or the student to the project group for decision-making.

This project organization, focused on the strategy development given in the example, is shown diagrammatically in Figure 9.2.

Working with project groups and work groups demands care. The progress and quality of the consultancy procedure become highly dependent on the input of others. This demands co-ordination and guidance. As a student, you can do the following:

- Draw up the objectives and work plan for each group and have them agreed
- Record the agreed dates for, and contents of, the interim and final reports

Figure 9.2
Model project organization for a consultancy project.

- Participate as a member of the different groups and provide help in arranging dates for group meetings and in the division of tasks
- Draw up the agenda for and take the minutes of group meetings
- Influence the composition of the groups to conform to high-quality guidelines with respect to knowledge, commitment, involvement, group size (three to five people) and authority within the organization
- Encourage each group to appoint a good chairman who will keep things moving, initially by deciding on all the meeting dates and the agreed milestones to be reached
- Prompt the project leaders to monitor progress on the agreed working plan and reports.

A critical success factor for a project group/work group approach is the speed at which the work is done. Too often, all sorts of mishaps lead to delays in the agreed execution of the work. In this way, enthusiasm is lost, the project loses momentum and eventually gets completely bogged down. This is why good planning, a fast working tempo, tight monitoring of progress, and a good example set by the student and the chairman are crucially important. A student can sustain this progress by acting as a 'prompter' where necessary, asking critical questions about progress and applying pressure by reminding people of agreements and deadlines.

We must pay further attention to one aspect of the composition of these groups, and that is opposition. It often happens that someone who is important for the project is not enthusiastic about the plans for tackling the specific issue. There can be various reasons for this. It is in some people's nature to always take an opposite view. It could also be that those concerned have genuine objections or see real risks, but others do not accept these because they view the situation from a different perspective. The natural tendency of people who want to make progress is to give opponents a minor role in the project or no role at all. After all, it is more agreeable to work with people who are enthusiastic. The argument for keeping someone out of the project may also be concern that this person will hold back the investigation. However understandable this tendency to keep an opponent on the sidelines may be, it does involve risks. Opponents who are excluded have no chance to contribute to the project. This only reinforces their scepticism, and if solutions are proposed, they are not their solutions and they will continue to oppose them. The more important their opinion is, the more they will be able to obstruct the project at the decision-making stage. It is better to assign them a responsible role in the investigation. Naturally, their scepticism will be reflected in the insistence on a thorough analysis and a critical evaluation of the alternatives. But in an environment in which the attitude is otherwise positive, this can only benefit the quality of the work. Attempts at sabotage by a chairman of a work group, for example, would be extremely conspicuous.[5]

The problem of coping with opposition should be recognized during this phase. Based on the activities during the orientation phase, it should be possible to assess where opposition to the project lies. Naturally, this will also be covered in Chapters 11 and 12, during the implementation.

In practice, students have a natural tendency towards the role of solo player. They must definitely be encouraged by their supervisors to include elements of the team player's role in their approach. You should not think in terms of either/or. In our experience, a 'mixed' approach is the most manageable, for both the student and the company. Too many work groups make the fieldwork project unnecessarily complex. But if the student can manage a small number of work groups for the main activities, this will be beneficial. In all cases, the main question is: How, as a student, can I organize the most effective consultancy process?

Consultation and reporting

It is always important to ensure that attention within the company remains focused on the consultancy project. This requires conscious effort, as otherwise the will to change and the level of interest die away quickly. Focus can be maintained by including a number of 'publicity' activities in the work programme, such as:

- Periodic presentations for those most directly concerned, including the management team
- Articles in the company magazine or newsletter on interesting findings and the progress of the project
- Working with work groups, as described above
- Platform group meetings

■ Keeping in contact with the most important decision-makers

■ Arranging interim milestones for decision-making.

In this way, people's attention will be kept focused on the consultancy project and everyone involved will be party to the final conclusions. It also means that the implementation of the recommendations will be a logical consequence of the process followed.

The structure of the in-depth investigation has been dealt with under 'Work planning', but the detailed planning of this was not discussed with the management team at the feedback session in Step 5. The management team only discussed the broad outline of the action plan. This is a good thing, as it is better to obtain agreement on the outline plan first, rather than go into details straight away. But the detailed plan must still be put forward for approval at some stage.

A method that has often proved to be successful is to include the detailed plan as an appendix with the report on the feedback session. Care should be taken that the correlation between the main outline that has already been discussed and the detailed plan is always clear. If the student can arrange to be present at the management team meeting when the documents are discussed to provide any necessary explanations, an excellent starting position will have been created for the in-depth research.

List of action points

Again, we conclude this phase in the consultancy process by summarizing the stages that must be worked through consecutively:

1 Define the issues to be investigated
2 Review the literature
3 Choose the methods of investigation
4 Choose the methods of data collection
5 Draw up a work plan
6 Obtain approval for the work plan
7 Choose the role to be played
8 Describe the project organization structure
9 Verify the level of support
10 Fill in the checklist
11 Consult the fieldwork supervisor.

Chapter notes

1. When those involved come to the conclusion, either right at the start or later during the orientation phase, that the project is in fact too extensive for one student to carry out all the steps, it is advisable to discuss the possibility of using the project that is about to start as a sub-project. In an 'overlap construction', a subsequent student might well be able to continue the work. See also Schaffer and Michaelson (1989: 5/2), who suggest working with sub-projects as building blocks for organizational change.

2. For drawing up a time plan for a consultancy project, see also S. Cosman, in Barcus and Wilkinson (1996: 13-2).

3. For example, see Lockyer and Gordon (1991).

4. Much has been written about the roles that consultants can choose in organizational consultancy work. In this book, we have chosen the roles that we consider to be most illustrative of the consultancy profession. For those who wish to look at the issue in more depth, the following references are given:

   ■ Greiner and Metzger (1983: 18) – types and roles of consultants
   ■ Nees and Greiner (1985: 68) – five types of organizational consultant
   ■ Lippitt and Lippitt (1994: 59) – eight roles
   ■ Champion *et al.* (1990) – role negotiations and choices
   ■ Williams and Woodward (1994: 52) – seven consultancy roles.

5. This approach is emphasized by the following excerpt from Greiner and Metzger (1983: 278):

   > One technique to prevent resistance is to 'co-opt' the naysayers before they become too vocal. You will receive hints at the data-gathering stage as to who the sceptics are. Those who are powerful can be won over by including them, not avoiding them in the planning of change. We have added them to the 'co-ordination committee' for the change programme. Or we have spent time with them informally, in going over our findings and listening to their reactions. A good catharsis of negative feelings can lead to a begrudging 'let's get on with it'. Also, a personal phone call from the CEO can win over a wavering executive.

See also Tjosvold (1991) for a description of an approach in which diversity can be made productive.

Exercises for Step 6

9.1   Dortmunder Hartmann AG

A comprehensive report on the problem of centralization/decentralization within the multinational machinery company, Dortmunder-Hartmann AG, is presented below.

In order to provide a thorough inventory of the problem, which has been under discussion for some time, a retired non-executive director has been asked to draw up a detailed list of all the relevant points. The documentation given below is the result of his work.

To help solve the problem, the company has decided to take you on as a fieldwork student. They have requested you not to repeat the inventory (orientation phase) as this would just be duplicated work. So you must proceed using the information already available. You decide that, since there has been no formal feedback presentation, you will at least present a detailed work plan to the people interviewed.

1   How would you summarize the problem situation? What is your diagnosis in terms of causes and effects? You will have to accept the fact that the director was unfamiliar with the TSP model and therefore his report is not drawn up in accordance with this.
2   Draw up the detailed work plan for the in-depth research. What role would you choose for carrying out the in-depth research?
3   Indicate the effect your choice of role has on the work plan you have drawn up.

Technical wholesale company Dortmunder-Hartmann AG

Dortmunder-Hartmann AG, with its head office in Dortmund (Germany), is a trading company in heavy equipment, machinery and other metal products for industry. It is one of the largest trading firms of this kind in the country. The management expect their sales to exceed €30 million this year.

The present company was formed two years ago when the owners of Hartmann AG bought 80 per cent of the shares in Dortmunder Maschinen Handel AG (DMH). The company name was changed at the same time. Now, all letterheads and name-plates on company property display the trademark DH in a diamond-shaped logo.

The company acts as agent for the sale of about 11 400 items within its product range. It also offers about 6000 items of its own. The products vary widely in value, from nuts and bolts sold for a small sum to air and gas compressors with prices ranging from €20 000 to 30 000 apiece. The company has subsidiaries in different European countries. These companies were acquired through takeovers of existing firms that already had a high reputation. Storage and sales take place at six branches: two in Dortmund and one each in Rotterdam, Billund (Denmark), Rennes (France) and Munich. At each of these sites, the company has extensive warehouse facilities and a sales staff who visit industrial companies that use the company's products.

At the time of the merger, the Dortmunder Maschinen Handel AG, which was founded by M. J. Frisch at the age of 28, had sales of €3.5 million via branches in Dortmund and Rennes. During the final ten years that DMH existed, sales increased by about 5 per cent, while during the same period, an economist active in this field estimated that sales in the sector as a whole had increased by 80 per cent. Frisch agreed with his wife and three children that it would be sensible to sell the company, as his heirs had no interest in taking an active role in the company. Now, at the age of 70, he says:

> I must say in all honesty that I had my hands completely full with Dortmund and Rennes. I could not have worked any harder, and I made a deliberate decision not to attempt to grow into an enormous company and achieve great things. My company had always made a good profit and I am proud of what I made it. When the company was sold, we had a turnover of €3.5 million and our personnel were well taken care of. This was necessary, as more than half of the 102 employees had worked for me for over 20 years.

Walther Fröhlich, Director of DH, says:

> The sale was a good thing both for Hartmann and for Frisch. The Non-Executive Board of Directors appointed me Managing Director of Hartmann ten years ago, with the firm conviction that we could grow substantially and profitably.

DMH sold more or less the same type of products in its two branches as we did, but we all realized that the company had become used to selling the same items to the same customers, and to handling the storage, financing and transport in the same way that it had always done. We knew that the turnover could be boosted considerably, and that its activities could be streamlined.

Fröhlich, now aged 49, saw the turnover of Hartmann rise from €10 to 20 million over a period of eight years before the merger, and the combined turnover of DH rise from €25 to 30 million in the two successive years. The owners of DH, five prominent businessmen from Dortmund who are active in the fields of banking and real estate, see Fröhlich as a man who is very well suited to his job. As one of them puts it:

His most positive characteristics are that he knows how to organize and to ensure that things run smoothly, and he actively looks for new opportunities to increase turnover and cut costs. He also understands the art of selecting good personnel, and that is what we need.

The branch in Rennes France

The branch in Rennes has been managed by Peter Straus for the past year. Straus, who is 45, worked for eleven years as business manager of the Dortmund branch of Hartmann. Shortly after becoming Director, Fröhlich recognized Straus's excellent managerial qualities, and he later decided that he was the ideal man to take over the management of the French branch and make something of it. Before the merger, turnover in Rennes had increased by about 5 per cent over ten years. The company sold industrial equipment, machines and building materials to local building firms, hardware stores, office buildings and schools. The profit was moderate, according to Straus.

When Straus took over in Rennes, Fröhlich drew up the job description shown below for the new job of general business manager in Rennes. He had visited Rennes several times to help settle minor difficulties; he spent two months there after becoming Director of DH and knows a great deal about how things are run there. Besides that, he says that he knows a lot about the Dortmund branch and that things are run there much as they are in Rennes. In Fröhlich's opinion, there are definitely aspects in Rennes that have potential for improvement:

Job description for the general manager of the Rennes branch

1 To be responsible for all the work carried out at the Rennes branch. In this capacity, given authority to ensure that all personnel carry out their duties as described.

2 To draw up a plan twice a year for sales and for expenditure and investments, so that all activities can be controlled in the branch and directed towards profitability.

3 To pay personal attention to the two primary activities that generate profit for DH: sales and handling goods. To draw up the policy rules and procedures necessary to carry out these activities effectively. To personally monitor these activities to ensure that the policy rules and procedures are followed.

4 To draw up task descriptions, policy rules and procedures for the activities of purchasing, personnel and stock management, keeping within the limits specified by the global company policy.

5 To select personnel for the branch, hire them and decide on the salaries to be paid.

6 To co-operate with the representatives of the head office in Dortmund when they visit the branch to gather information for the company policy and for higher level decisions.

The purchasing and personnel responsibilities, for example, have never been clearly described. Both Straus and I will need to do something about this one of these days. He has made a number of proposals, but we are not in complete agreement about purchasing. He wants the branch to have the authority to purchase all the items it carries except for items costing more than €5000 each and items bought in quantities less than that on which we receive the maximum bulk discount. In other words, if Rennes orders enough bolts to be eligible for the discount on its own, they would not need permission from us. But I fear that this will lead to excessive stocks being maintained there, with too much money being tied up. It is also detrimental to DH's image if suppliers perceive that our major orders are not dealt with centrally. In fact, one of Straus's weak points is his stock management. On my bimonthly visits to Rennes,

I check through the stock levels of the 400 fastest-moving items with his bookkeeper. Although I have no evidence to prove this, I believe that either the quantities he orders are too large, or he is too cautious with delivery times and submits the orders far too early. I tell Straus this each time, but up to now, he only wishes to be bound by the two rules I mentioned previously. We need to work out a satisfactory policy for this, because meticulous stock management is one of the ways to turn a profit in this business. His ratio of stock to sales is less productive than those of Hamburg or Munich.

Specific activities in Rennes

Two weeks ago, Fröhlich received a number of proposals from P. Schneider, the stock and purchasing manager of DH. In Schneider's view, these proposals should be implemented in all branches to ensure that capital tied up in stock and related risks are kept to a minimum. These proposals are summarized below.

Proposal for stock management within Dortmunder-Hartmann AG

The objective of stock management within DH is to make the costs of storage, insurance and interest lower than those of our competitors and to reduce the risk of damage and ageing.

Once every six months (or once a year if the branches react unfavourably to this period), each branch will be required to produce an inventory of all items whose value (price × quantity in stock) exceeds €400. Of the 5000–6000 items handled by the average branch, about 1500 will come into this category. The following information must be given for each of these items:

Name of the item, code, quantity in stock, quantity sold over the last 12 months, anticipated delivery time.

Schneider was trained in technical subjects. During the past year, he has taken two courses on operational research and has made use of books and magazine articles to study mathematical methods of stock management. He claims that linear programming and other OR methods will be extremely valuable for DH, although it will be at least five years before these techniques can be applied within the company.

In the field of personnel affairs, DH has recruited two staff officers to plan the HR policy and its implementation across the entire company. The view is that this will give DH a substantial advantage over their competitors as a result of greater co-operation between their personnel, with lower staff turnover and therefore less damage to items during receipt and storage. The management considers that this will also help combat carelessness and theft.

C. Kaufmann, the personnel manager, has prepared a draft policy manual setting out about 45 policy rules and procedures. One of these is that the head office will send a personnel officer to each of the branches once a year, with the objective of working with the branch manager to agree the salary bands for all employees at that branch.

The focus on sales in Rennes proves to be extremely successful. The merger appears to have given the four salesmen new interest in their work and their sales have increased by 12 per cent since the previous year, when Straus came to Rennes. However, nobody knows exactly why this has happened. Fröhlich would very much like to know this as he hopes to achieve the same result in the other branches. Straus attributes the success primarily to Fröhlich:

> I know a great deal about sales, but I have always been involved in operations, both when I was branch manager for Hartmann in Dortmund and before that, when I worked for the external service department in Dortmund and in Munich. I hold a meeting with my salesmen once a month and examine their plans for the following month (new customers, routes, number of visits, items to call attention to, etc.). Fröhlich not only worked out the present remuneration system, which I believe to be one of the reasons for our sales success, but he talks to the salesmen and helps them draw up the plans that I review with them two weeks later.
>
> In fact, I realize that the word 'help' is an understatement. Fröhlich even goes so far as deciding on their routes if he is not satisfied with the number of customers visited or the places visited. He also tells them whether salesmen in other branches sell more than they do, and what techniques they use. In any case, the salesmen seem to be happy with this, sales are increasing and I would not be able to manage without this assistance. He sometimes brings Dick Braun with him, a man I knew for years when he was a first-rate salesman in Dortmund. It is rumoured in Dortmund that Dick will be given a new job as sales manager for the entire company, and will take over the type of work that Fröhlich does now in this field.

Apparently the salesmen have differing views on the value of Fröhlich's help. Two of them say that he has helped them a great deal, although they have also found Straus helpful. Two others, however, say that Fröhlich was unfamiliar with the region around

Rennes and that he was unreasonable because he was unaware of various obstacles and difficulties in certain parts of that region. 'It all looks the same to him on the map.'

Fröhlich claims to be fervently in favour of decentralization. In his view, nothing else lightens the burden on a Director as much, while at the same time encouraging people to work hard and efficiently. In Rennes, the decentralization idea specifically concerns the four operational departments: receipt of goods, internal transport, storage, and dispatch. Straus has drawn up a job description for the heads of each of these departments. During visits to Rennes, however, nobody from Dortmund ever has any reason to talk about the work done by these people. Straus makes a trip around the warehouses at least once a week to make suggestions about the storage of particular items ('we need a lower shelf for these fittings, closer to the door, as they have a high turnover') and he formulates his own storage rules ('never put inflammable items in the eastern section of the building'). According to Straus, it is correct and proper that instructions are received from Dortmund on subjects such as the type of equipment used for transport, and that an analyst must draw up the working procedures for every person in the warehouses. These matters are recorded in instruction booklets, but Straus points out that nobody from Dortmund ever checks that the instructions are complied with. Straus does follow some of these instructions, but not all of them. Fröhlich has told him privately that once the effect of the merger has manifested itself in other areas, it will be necessary for someone to monitor the consistency of working methods in all branches, otherwise there is a risk that the advantages of working at low costs based on a study of methods will be lost.

Budgets for day-to-day costs and capital outlays

The only point on which Straus seriously disagrees with the head office concerns the budget. Fröhlich has insisted on the following procedure:

The managers of the branches (except for those in Rotterdam and Dortmund) must produce a budget drawn up on the basis of a form sent to them from Dortmund, on which all the items of expenditure in the branch are specified under about 40 headings. Twice a year, Dortmund will provide the branches with a projection of the total sales for that sector in each sales area. Each manager must examine this projection, in relation to his own observations and the percentage of the total sales for the sector that DH would expect to achieve, and draw up a sales target. With this sales target in mind, the branch manager then estimates the sums required for each of the 40 expenditure categories (newspaper advertisements, salaries of sales personnel, cost of receiving goods, other salary categories, etc.). There are six categories (such as stocks, other floating assets and buildings) that indicate where capital outlay is necessary. For each capital category other than floating assets, every project must be specified, irrespective of size.

Straus has strongly objected to having to draw up a budget for 40 expenditure categories every six months. He has said repeatedly that as long as his profits are satisfactory as a percentage of the sales and as a percentage of the investments, Dortmund need not concern itself with the individual components of this result. In other words, 'If the percentages are good, why worry about whether this is due to increased turnover, lower costs or whatever.'

Fröhlich, on the other hand, has three or four examples where branch managers either requested investment in projects that did not make sufficient profit or wanted to incur costs that were not necessary for running the branch smoothly. He says:

> We need more understanding of the global picture than we can get solely from the profit figures, as otherwise, however well managers may be doing their job, they tend to place too much emphasis on their own activities and are not objective enough. It is nonsense, for example, for Straus to ask for an extra man for dispatch. He is under so much pressure from the personnel in that department that he really thinks that this extra man is needed. If we were not supporting him, he would have to give in to this pressure. This means we must either make alterations to the budget or regulate the use of extra personnel for dispatch. Naturally, Straus does not find this pleasant, but it is for his benefit in the long run.

Chapter 10

Step 7: In-depth research

In moving from Step 6 to Step 7, we leave behind the orientation phase and proceed to the research and solution phase. The orientation phase focused entirely on arriving at a good starting position for an effective consultancy process. The investigation contract must now be carried out and produce solutions for the specific problem. A working plan has been drawn up and approved, and will act as a guideline.

There are so many different types of fieldwork project that it is impossible to study them individually and give specific instructions for each. For example, an assignment to reduce the stocks held by a wholesale company requires a completely different research approach from an assignment to develop a marketing plan for a new type of photocopier paper. For this reason, we will restrict ourselves in this chapter to a number of themes that generally apply, such as:

- Formulating the research questions
- Choosing methods for collecting and analysing information
- Dealing with a number of problems that occur frequently
- Supervising work groups.

Before we start, a completed checklist for Step 7 is shown in Table 10.1. This checklist does not give details of the extensive research process. The project planning described in Step 6 is the guideline. The objective is to at least obtain the information required to reach satisfactory solutions. The completed checklist is taken from a fieldwork study by a student in an R&D organization. To make sure the answers are properly understood,

Table 10.1

Example of a completed logbook page for Step 7

Checklist – Step 7: In-depth research	
Questions	**Answers**
1 What is the research model for this project?	• Three orientations (see Figure 10.1)
2 What data collection methods did you use?	• Interviews, documentation review, participation in meetings of discipline groups
3 What are the research results so far?	• The three orientations can be combined in an approach that fits in with the specs; an initial draft has been delivered both for the generic and for the specific aspects
4 On which points was there divergence from the project planning?	• It was decided to use one instead of two pilot groups
5 What interim feedback has been given, to whom and with what results?	• Interim meetings with sounding board group: four discipline group leaders, and a meeting with the managing director of the R&D organization: commitment on the approach, support for the idea of writing a piece in the personnel publication, agreement that people who take part in the work group may do this during working hours
6 What possible solutions have emerged from the investigation?	• Make a quick start in the pilot group; make interim reports to other groups; limit this project to the development of indicators and start looking for a student to pick up the baton for the following stage
7 Which people are for and against the various solutions?	• No problems observed as yet
8 Which solution is the most feasible and why?	• The first drafts were received reasonably favourably. We now need to maintain 'momentum'
9 Who are the most powerful 'sponsors' of the project?	• The director of the R&D organization is becoming more and more enthusiastic
10 Remarks	

we also provide some concise background information about the project.

A business administration student is carrying out a fieldwork project in the R&D organization of a large international company. The purpose of this organization is to develop ideas for new products and transfer them to one of the business units of the parent company. The R&D organization is composed of discipline groups. These discipline groups supply resources (the time and effort of their members) to project leaders who are responsible for developing innovations. The activities of the personnel are supervised in two ways: via their own discipline group and via the project teams in which they are working. It is therefore a matrix organization.

Within the R&D organization, importance has always been placed on developing and improving methods and techniques for ensuring that the projects run as successfully as possible. To this end, there is a detailed innovation and project management system.

Much less attention is paid to the operation of the discipline groups. It is their task to assist the project leaders by providing personnel with high-level specialist knowledge. It is left up to the individual groups to decide how they will do this: via conference visits, guest speakers, internal seminars, literature reviews, collaboration with external institutions, etc.

The management of the R&D organization is increasingly questioning the wisdom of leaving the supervision of the discipline groups entirely to themselves. A meeting was held with all the group leaders, in which the concerns of the management were expressed. The problem was generally accepted. However, all those present recognized that they were too busy to spare time for such a potentially large-scale project.

The assignment for the fieldwork student is to contribute towards the intended internal organizational changes. Performance indicators must be developed for the discipline groups, with a dual purpose. The groups must be able to use these criteria to make and implement plans for maintaining their high-level specialist knowledge and improving it where necessary. The criteria must also act as a guideline for reports to the management of the R&D organization.

During his feedback session, the student reported that there seemed to be support for the development of performance indicators. The reason that some groups are more enthusiastic than others is primarily down to differences in workloads. People are worried that the development of performance indicators will require a great deal of time and effort. But there are at least two groups that are prepared to spearhead the process. The others will follow.

A work plan has been agreed in which the student will develop the detailed programme of requirements for the proposed approach. He will base the approach on literature relating to organizational learning, performance management and knowledge management, and he will make a start with two of the eight discipline groups (pilot groups). Table 10.1 shows an interim report to the fieldwork supervisor on the in-depth investigation that is under way. The answers indicate that material is being drawn from three theoretical orientations:

1. From the literature on organizational learning, the student concluded that in order to learn, groups and individuals need certain 'organizational routines'. If work processes are continuously being changed, people cannot acquire useful experience. However, these routines should not be set in stone because in that scenario there is no 'address' for people's innovation and improvement ideas. This raises the question of what kind of routines this particular organization has and whether these routines support or hamper learning.[1]

2. Study of the literature on knowledge management suggested looking into the possibility of using the concepts of knowledge creation and knowledge sharing in this professional R&D environment. It raised the question of whether this organization consciously pays attention to knowledge management issues. If it is lagging behind, this could also be a cause of the problem.[2]

3. The literature on performance management appeared to cover two schools of thought. The first promotes a top-down approach. The Balanced Score Card is the best known example of this approach. The second stream advocates a bottom-up perspective, and builds on research indicating that people perform better and are more motivated if they are involved in defining the performance levels they have to achieve. The student wanted to combine the two approaches such that each discipline group would use a number of generic and a

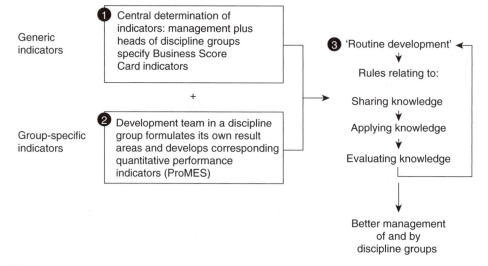

Figure 10.1
Appendix to in-depth investigation: research model.

number of group-specific indicators. These common and group-specific indicators can be used to help improve performance management.[3]

The research model is as shown in Figure 10.1.

The student works with two teams: one with representatives from all six discipline groups to specify the performance indicators common to all the groups (filling in the Balanced Score Card) and a second in which members of one discipline group formulate the specific indicators for this group. Both teams have drawn up their first draft.

It is important that the student has recorded several different options for solutions. Later on in the book (Step 8), the advantages of this will be considered in more depth. The other questions and answers relate to the feasibility of the solution. The key point is that any solution chosen must be possible to implement.

Formulation of the research questions

The assignment for the fieldwork project is formulated during the feedback session. There is also discussion on the end product to be generated by the project: what should be achieved when the student has finished. In our view, the end product of a fieldwork project should be an implemented solution, i.e. an organizational change.

The first task is to decide what information is necessary to successfully complete the assignment. In other words, what research questions must be asked and answered? These questions are derived from the research model used. The research model summarizes and classifies the information that must be collected in order to find a solution for the specific problem. You could call a research model a disposable item[4] created for a specific management problem. The function of the model is to control the process of data collection in a particular investigation. Once the model is no longer required, it can be discarded. When deciding which factors are important and how these variables are related, several sources are used:

- General theoretical knowledge that the student has acquired by studying various subjects during his or her academic course
- Specific conjectures and assumptions about how things work in this company, based on the orientation that has already taken place
- Other people's knowledge and experience gained by consulting experts in both this company and in the academic environment, and by examining other students' reports of similar problems in the same company or elsewhere.

Methods of collecting and analysing information

Once it is clear what needs to be investigated, it must be decided *how* the required information will be collected. There are various methods of collecting information. The researcher must weigh up the pros and cons of each method and decide which is best.[5] It is practically impossible to give general guidelines for doing this. The important point for the student to bear in mind is that the research results must be 'solid' enough to back up the proposals for organizational changes. The student's research results must stand up to claims that they are 'only' the researcher's subjective impressions. In most cases, people will try to work as objectively as possible during the research.

But the words 'as objectively as possible' imply a certain degree of relativity. 'Pure objectiveness' cannot always be achieved within the time available and with the capacity and resources available.

The information a consultant or fieldwork student needs to answer his or her research questions can generally be collected in five ways:

1 Participation
2 Interviews
3 Observations
4 Documents
5 Measurements.

We will consider each of these methods in turn.

Participation

Students generally spend most of their time at the company during the fieldwork period, have a room there, take part in the informal routine of coffee, lunch and tea breaks, and see and hear for themselves how the organization operates. To get a good picture of the problem situation and the options for solving it, it is important to participate in the more formal routines: to be present at the departmental work meetings and project team meetings, or to accompany one or more employees during their work. We have already pointed out how useful it is to observe the operation of the company's primary business processes during the orientation stage. For the in-depth research, these forms of participation do not directly provide objective facts, but these contacts can be used to verify data and ideas, and to improve your knowledge of the people you will be working with as a fieldwork student. They can also give you a better understanding of company customs that will be relevant to your consultancy project.

A few examples of the latter are:

■ Meetings where definite decisions are never taken, if your recommendations as a student will be dependent on that decision-making process later on
■ Wasteful practices, if you are engaged in a cost-cutting programme

- Unfriendly telephone manner to customers, if your field-work project is concerned with improving customer relations
- A dominant manager who barely allows other people to speak, if you have been instructed to draw up a strategy based on participation.

Such insights are by no means always the result of interviews or other methods of collecting information. This is why participation in the company's business processes is extremely important. It makes timely discussion of these phenomena possible, so that you can take advantage of this in carrying out your fieldwork assignment.

Interviews

Interviews are commonly used in fieldwork projects. An interview is a flexible method of gaining understanding of a problem and obtaining ideas for possible solutions. We have already discussed several aspects of the interview in Chapter 6 (Step 3: Orientational interviews). In addition, it can be beneficial to interview people from outside the company, particularly in connection with the in-depth research. The most obvious choices are the subject supervisors from your own educational establishment. If they can add to your knowledge of the sector in which your fieldwork project is taking place, this is certainly an advantage. But supervisors can also provide information about models, concepts and working methods relating to strategy, marketing, product organization, support processes or logistic processes in which they are specialized. Another category of people who may have useful information to help you in your in-depth research is the business specialists. The company itself, the business association, the Chamber of Commerce, the bank or the company's accountant can help you to find them and may be able to open doors for an interview.

Observations

Observation is a suitable method of acquiring information that is not recorded in writing. The basic idea is that the consultant or student watches how things work in a systematic fashion. Case 10.1 demonstrates how this method can be used in a fieldwork project.

Case 10.1

A student was carrying out a fieldwork project for a large car dealer. One of the problems was that mechanics had to wait for components from the storeroom when they needed them in the course of their work. This waiting time had not been taken into account in the benchmark times drawn up for carrying out various tasks. At varying times over several days, the student logged the time that mechanics had to wait before being served by the storeroom manager. Her observations were used to modify the benchmark times and subsequently to reduce the waiting times.

What types of observations can be made? A long list of possible items for observation could be drawn up, but we will limit ourselves to a few of them:

- *Technical aspects.* Examples are known of professional technical consultants who can walk through a factory and give a reasonable assessment of the extent to which efficiency can be improved solely on the basis of what they have seen. A student who acted in this way would not be taken seriously. It is more sensible to follow the method used by the student in Case 10.1. Observation means watching and recording:

  - drawing the layout of the shopfloor, storerooms, offices
  - noting which machines are not running, and at which times, without an obvious reason
  - recording the bottlenecks in the production process – in other words, where people have to wait for each other before they can continue their work
  - registering how many products are rejected during the production process and what happens to these rejected products.

- *Organizational aspects.* Organizational aspects relate to the behaviour of individuals and groups:

  - registering what people do when there is an interruption in the production process

- noting how the agreed quality controls are carried out
- determining how many changes to the production planning are made during particular periods
- observing how information issued by the central management is communicated to the work floor
- noting whether personnel comply with safety regulations at particular times.

There is a lot to see within a company. However, not everything is worth recording. As a student, you must be guided by your research questions. Moreover, the methods to be used must be agreed with your principal. If you agree that these include carrying out a number of observations, it is important that those who will be observed are informed. Most people do not feel comfortable with someone looking over their shoulder. This means the student must act circumspectly. Those involved must be aware of the purpose of the observations. It must be clear to everyone that it is not a question of judging their work, but of obtaining a reliable picture of the way activities take place. In most cases, a discussion with the people involved will help to ensure their co-operation, giving them the chance to explain what they do, why they do it and what they would like changed. It is important that the people observed act normally, and do not try to work faster or slower, better or worse. If something out of the ordinary occurs, the question of whether this information should be included in the observation report should be discussed.

Documents

This covers data that the organization collects itself for internal or external purposes. In most cases, organizations have a great deal of information available that can be interesting and important for the student. Every production company has technical information about product specifications, material use, hours worked, processing times, adjustment times, etc. Commercially important information is frequently available too: purchasing and sales records, customer information with invoicing details, delivery times, complaints records. Usually, this information covers a long period of time, so that trends over that period can be followed. The personnel department has information on the recruitment, selection and training of personnel, and on turnover and absence from work. In addition, almost all companies have reports or memos on their strategy, long-term plans and annual reports that show the company's vision of the present and the future.

In many cases, it is possible to collect this information, but a warning is necessary. Not all the information obtained in this way is reliable. For example, information on machine stoppage, defects, rejects or stock levels is not always accurate. The way the organization actually operates often deviates from what is recorded in schedules, procedures, systems and instructions. It is important for the student to examine the information obtained critically, if possible to compare it with similar departments or companies, and if necessary to check it by further investigation.

Besides this available information, other information that has not yet been recorded is often needed for carrying out the assignment. This occurs more often than people realize, and there is a reason for this. In areas where an organization wishes to introduce corrections and improvements, insufficient attention has usually been paid to the underlying cause of the problem. For example, loss of customers can be explained by complaints that have not been properly dealt with, but also not measured. Machine stoppages only receive attention – and are measured – when production losses become significant. This is why crucial data often still needs to be collected in consultancy and fieldwork projects. We pointed this out during the orientation phase, and encouraged you to find out during the orientational interviews what relevant information is unavailable, or not available in the appropriate format. This makes it possible to initiate the process of collecting, registering and sorting information in good time, so that it is available for carrying out the in-depth research. The same applies if omissions in the available information are discovered in the course of the in-depth research. This may cause some loss of time, but this is not necessarily a disaster for fieldwork projects covering a reasonably long period.

Such registration activities are generally suitable for delegation to people involved in the relevant work processes, which can save the student considerable time. But it is important to draw up good working instructions for these people, accompanied if appropriate by schedules, descriptions of the data required, the units in which the data should be expressed, registration frequency, etc. In order to compare the results with information available for the sector as a whole, it is sensible to take into account the format in which this is available.

Measurements

A measurement may be necessary if the information sought is not available in writing and cannot be collected by means of observations or interviews. An existing measurement tool can sometimes be used. If this is not possible, a measurement tool must be designed and used. Depending on the questions that need to be answered, there are two types of measurement tool students can use: a survey and a technical measurement procedure.

Surveys

A survey is an ideal method for questioning a number of people systematically.[6] In consultancy and fieldwork projects, the limited time available means that it is not always possible to interview everybody who might provide useful information. One reason for carrying out a survey is that a large number of people can be questioned. An interview can easily take an hour and a half, with another hour to process the results. If the number of people to be questioned is large (more than 20), then you should ask yourself whether another method of collecting information would not be more efficient. The interview method can also be a problem when people are separated by a considerable distance – for example, at different branches of a company. Another reason for carrying out a survey is to ask standard questions, so that the results can be summarized afterwards as statistics for the total group and for subgroups, with frequencies, averages and distributions. This is important for areas such as market research.

The survey method is mostly used in research covering a large number of individuals. The entire group is sometimes approached, but a random sample of the population may also be used. In a relatively large group, it may be useful to process the results statistically – for example, when measuring satisfaction within a company department. There are several types of survey. A few of the most common ones are mentioned below.

■ *Telephone survey*. The student phones the respondents, asks the questions from a questionnaire and records the answers directly in the questionnaire. This is the most frequently used method for large-scale research. A large number of people can be covered in a short time. The response rate is generally high (80 per cent on average). This tool is very suitable for market research.

■ *Written survey*. A carefully drawn up questionnaire is sent to the respondents by internal or external post. The respondents are asked to complete the questionnaire and return it before a specified date. The response rate is usually between 40 and 80 per cent. Within a company, the response rate to a questionnaire of this type can be favourably influenced by enclosing a letter of recommendation from the principal and/or by distributing the questionnaire personally and then collecting it again later on.

■ *Group survey*. It is sometimes possible to gather the personnel of a department together to fill in the questionnaire.

Surveys are widely used, but the results are sometimes disappointing. It is frequently much more difficult to process and interpret the results than the compiler expects. We will cover a few quality requirements that a survey should satisfy:

■ Do not use difficult words. Every respondent should easily be able to understand what is being asked.

■ Avoid negatives. Do not use words such as 'not', 'none', 'never'. Sentences containing negatives almost always lead to misunderstandings.

■ In questions about actions in the past (how often did you ...?), always specify clearly the time period that is referred to.

■ In the choices of answer, avoid words such as 'sometimes', 'now and then', 'often' and 'a lot'. All the respondents will use different standards.

The success of a survey can be improved by carrying out a pilot: ask a few of those involved to fill in the questionnaire, ask for their comments and use their scores in preparation for processing the rest of the results.

Technical measurement procedures

When reliable information is needed about the properties or performance of technical systems, measurement tools will frequently be used to record factors such as pressure, temperature or quantity at different times. This is the case when no measurement results are available at all, and when results are available but need to be checked for accuracy.

We will mention a few situations in which technical measurements are used:

- Goods flow management – stock levels, machine processing times
- Quality – rejects, waste, quality variations, customer complaints, safety (accidents)
- Production equipment – maintenance state, energy and water consumption
- Commercial administration – decision points in the tendering process, market segmentation
- Personnel administration – absence due to sickness.

Analysis from the outside in

An important principle is that most problems within organizations are caused by changing circumstances outside the organization. The consequence is that the norm for aberrations must be set outside the organization. A student can calculate stock levels and machine times, study the level of satisfaction with a new information-processing system, determine the efficiency of the tendering procedure, etc., but for each of these research activities, the question of what is normal must be answered. How high should stock levels be? How much machine stoppage is acceptable? What should we do if personnel are dissatisfied with the new system? How long should you continue spending time and effort on tenders with a meagre chance of success? The norms must be found outside the organization, in the status of the market in which the company is active. What do the customers want? How does our performance compare with that of competitors?

The analysis – deciding whether the research results obtained fall within the norm or not – must be performed from the outside in. This means that externally directed performance indicators must be used. The most important ones are quality, price, flexibility, delivery times and delivery reliability. A successful company should be among the best in its market for one or more of these indicators.

Analysing from the outside in means that the relevant business processes are examined on the basis of the defined performance indicators. Deviations are noted and converted into improvement targets.

An analysis by a student working at a machinery factory showed that the primary customer requirement was that components were delivered within 24 hours. The company could not always meet this requirement, while competitors succeeded in doing so. In a case like this, the improvement targets to be set are clear.

Coping with several common problems

In practice, the research does not always proceed according to plan. We will cover a number of points that are important for keeping the research on course.

Keep hold of the purpose of the project

Even after a carefully executed orientation phase, unexpected developments arise in almost every project which make it necessary to modify the original work plan. If, after critical evaluation, this is really unavoidable, then make sure that the final objective of the assignment remains the guideline for any changes made to the approach.

Maintain contact with the principal

In the heat of the research activities, it is easy to neglect contact with the principal. An informal chat every now and again ensures that focus on the project does not diminish.

Communicate formally and informally with all parties

This includes people such as the chairmen of the project and work groups, platform group, decision-makers and opinion leaders. By doing this, you will retain a good picture of how the project is regarded and how it is progressing.

Record important changes to the planning and progress of the project

Sending these reports to those involved in the project means that it will always be possible to refer back to them. This will prevent misunderstandings and communication breakdowns. Do not forget to keep the fieldwork supervisor informed as well. He can help to steer matters in the right direction if necessary.

Keep a project dossier containing important project information

In a consultancy project of any size, a quantity of paperwork can soon accumulate, such as:

- Interview reports
- Survey results
- Progress reports
- Process descriptions
- Minutes of meetings.

It is only possible to keep track of these by filing them according to subject and with a clear list of contents. A suspension file system is a useful accessory. In projects involving work groups, the work group chairmen should also each keep a dossier. A good way of introducing dossier discipline in work groups is to issue ring binders with subject-based tab pages.

Try to attend meetings where decisions about the project will be taken

Management teams, steering committees and suchlike make decisions that affect the progress and results of the consultancy project. If you ask to attend these in person you will be able to prevent inaccurate ideas from developing and you can do your best to make sure that the right decisions are taken. Moreover, you will then know at first hand what is being done with the research results.

Monitor efficiency during the project execution

The collection of information can come up against unexpected difficulties. You need to make sure that effort is not being wasted on relatively unimportant details. The amount of work and its relative importance must always be weighed up in the context of the overall research objectives.

Maintain momentum

Long periods of inactivity will lead to loss of focus and will reduce the project's prospects of success. There is also the risk that the time available for the fieldwork project will run out.

Always produce your important reports as verbal presentations with the help of slides in the first instance

Presentations force you to define the essence of the report and therefore will focus the discussion on the key themes. A written report can be drawn up afterwards if this is desirable.

Maintain good contact with the company coach and the fieldwork supervisor

Regular contact ensures that the company requirements and the course requirements do not become too widely separated.

List of action points

We conclude by summarizing the process steps that must be carried out:

1 Formulate the research questions
2 Choose methods of collecting and analysing information
3 Monitor progress
4 Consult the platform group
5 Modify the project
6 Manage the dossier
7 Answer the research questions
8 Produce interim reports

9   Complete the checklist
10 Consult the fieldwork supervisor.

Chapter notes

1   Some references on organizational learning: Argyris and Schön (1996); Moorman and Miner (1997); Crossan *et al.* (1999).

2   For more on knowledge management, see Majchrzak *et al.* (2004).

3   Some references on performance measurement: Kaplan and Norton (1996); Van Tuijl (1997).

4   For those who are interested in the methodological background, there are many additional sources – for example, Jankowicz (2000) and Saunders (2002).

5   The practical collection and processing of data in a consultancy project is described by Greiner and Metzger (1983: 218).

6   For guidelines on the design, processing and reporting of surveys, see Fink (1995a–c) and Dillman (2000).

Exercises for Step 7

10.1   Research questions

The in-depth research includes many questions to which the answers must be sought through focused investigation. For each of the questions given below, show in the form of a brief work plan how you would try to discover the answers required.

1   A company wants to find out the following information about a competitor:

- its turnover for the last financial year
- its profit for the last financial year
- the average stock of finished product (expressed as a sum of money) during the last financial year
- the average production losses caused by rejects.

2   A company wants to know how many competitors it has in the country.
3   A company wants to know the scale of exports in its own field throughout the country.
4   A company wants to know how its delivery reliability compares with that of its four most important competitors.
5   A company wants to know what the best number of staff for its external sales department should be.
6   A company wants to know how best to distribute tasks between the external and the internal sales departments.
7   A principal wants to know what the working climate in his company is.
8   A company wants to know how satisfied its 500 customers are.
9   A company wants to know whether its own distribution department is cheaper than the services of an external distributor.
10 A company wants to know how to weigh up the advantages and disadvantages of central and non-central sales of its merchandise.

10.2   Work planning

The following text comes from a fieldwork report:

> Company X wishes to deliver to its major customers (20) within two days of receiving an order, and to its smaller customers (150) within a week. By doing this, it aims to be seen as the fastest supplier by the customers while keeping its stock costs as low as possible.

1   Draw up a detailed work plan to measure the extent to which this target is met.
2   Design the necessary questionnaires, forms, etc.

10.3   Stagnation during in-depth research

What causes of stagnation during the in-depth research can you think of, and what measures can you take to prevent and/or eliminate these to maintain momentum?

10.4   Units Ltd

The company Units Ltd manufactures, sells and lets units for temporary accommodation. The company started out as an ordinary carpentry firm supplying doors, window frames and other woodwork for the building industry. But 20 years ago, owner/director Dan Vernon had the idea of switching to the construction of units. He designed several models himself, produced a sales leaflet and renamed the company Units Ltd. After a slow start, the new commercial activities started to pick up. With the assistance of Dan's advertising campaign, prospective customers discovered that the units could not only be used as building site huts, but that, with a suitable assembly system, schools, homes for the elderly and even factory offices could make use of them. Notably, if new building work was taking a long time (industry) or government money was not yet available for building (schools, geriatric care), a construction based on standard units could fill the gap, even for a period of several years. It became less common for customers to actually buy the units; renting was generally preferred. Thus, Units Ltd became a major operator in wooden unit rentals. The 'carpentry division' limited its activities to maintenance and repairs and to building new units as required.

During the good years, the company turnover rose to about €50 million (rental income) with a staff of about 300. As a modern businessman, Vernon set up a works council and a non-executive board at an early stage. He considered the former important because the welfare of his personnel was one of his priorities, and he did not want to lose 'the voice of the shopfloor' as a result of the increasing scale. The non-executive board fitted in with his wish to ensure that there would be people to look after the company if anything happened to him.

In recent years, the company seems to have lost its way. Turnover has stagnated, more competition has appeared and even regular customers are turning their backs on the company. The results are also showing a negative trend, which worries the non-executive board and the bank. Vernon, who is now nearly 60, has realized that a change of direction may be needed to get the company back on course again. In consultation with the non-executive board, he decided to take on a commercial assistant director, who can take over from Vernon if he proves suitable. Leo Karsten was the man found for this purpose. Leo worked for a building firm with which Vernon had a good relationship, and the two men always got on well. When Karsten made it clear during one of their conversations that he was available, Dan Vernon did not hesitate for long before making him an offer. With the approval of the non-executive board and the works council, the matter was soon settled.

Within just a few months, it became clear to Karsten, with his feeling for business, that the company was not doing well. Naturally, this had been hinted at during the recruitment procedure, but the reality appeared to be even gloomier. For this reason, he suggested to Vernon that they should take on a student for a fieldwork project to examine the situation in more depth. Anna Verdegaal was recruited from a neighbouring college of economics. She had read *Business Research Projects* and was determined to put into practice what she had learnt. Up to now, she has done this successfully. She has now reached the solution phase of her assignment, but sees a complication looming.

Looking back on her work so far, she realizes that Units Ltd is in deep trouble. Her research indicates that while the company was resting on its former reputation, several competitors had the idea of marketing units constructed of man-made material with aluminium frames. These units have the advantage that maintenance costs are low and they can therefore be rented more cheaply. In addition, the units are assembled using a very simple system, which also keeps the rental prices down. Finally, the insulation of the units is much better, so that the interior temperature in the summer is more comfortable, while fuel costs are lower in the winter. So without anyone realizing it, Vernon's units have become hopelessly outdated, but the rocketing demand from the market prevented Vernon from recognizing this for a long time. Now that demand is stabilizing, Units Ltd is experiencing problems. Vernon can only keep going by offering rock-bottom prices, but the position is still extremely uncertain. Anna is considering two possible options for solving the problems. One consists of a U-turn approach. This would mean reducing the personnel by a third, splitting off a number of activities and attempting to obtain the licence for the Dutch market from a Belgian manufacturer of modern units. She knows Karsten has a preference for this approach, as he believes that only fast intervention can save the company. The second option is more conservative. No more jobs would be lost than the reduction due to natural wastage. A team from the technical department would be instructed to design a series of modern units, which would gradually replace the old wooden units. Vernon is strongly in favour of this option. In his view, the company is financially capable of surviving this gradual change. Over the course of various meetings and interim reports, Anna has realized how the two directors are thinking. Although each shows respect for the other's opinions, their preferences for the course to be followed clearly differ.

1 Who should preferably be Anna's principal and why?
2 How should she determine the best option, or is this unnecessary? Explain your answer.
3 Could Anna have prevented this stalemate and, if so, how?
4 Describe an approach for obtaining the unanimous support of both directors for a single solution.

Chapter 11

Step 8: Solution plan

In the TSP, the processes of carrying out the research and drawing up the solution plan are closely interlinked. The two steps together have a cyclic character in the TSP schedule. During the in-depth research, information becomes available that contains the outlines of solutions. A good consultant will regularly communicate these developments to the relevant people and organizations, to ensure that the final recommendation will both have the desired result and be achievable.

We regard the research activities and the search for a solution as a cyclic process. By 'cyclic', we mean that the quality of possible solutions can be tested in a number of cycles until a suitable solution is found. In carrying out the research, ideas for possible solutions emerge. These solutions prompt new, supplementary questions that need answers. Some solutions will be dropped, others will be refined and modified.[1]

The research phase is nearing its end when several reasonable solutions have been identified. The advantages and disadvantages of these solutions must be sufficiently understood to allow for sound decision-making. This is the function of Step 8: organizing the decision-making process so that the best of the proposed solutions can be chosen based on the research results. The activities of the consultant or fieldwork student include:

- Preparing a clear presentation explaining the possible solutions that have been identified and the information on which they are based. Criteria for choosing a solution must be proposed, along with the solutions that are preferred by the student based on these criteria. A degree of insight into the organizational consequences of each option can provide considerable assistance in the selection process.

- Communicating the solution plan, in the presence of the management, to other bodies, such as the works council, if requested to do so.
- Carrying out further small-scale research to answer unanticipated questions.
- Pressing for quick decision-making in order to expedite the implementation activities.

An example of a completed checklist for Step 8 is shown in Table 11.1. The assignment described here was to advise a plastics factory how to improve its response to its customers' wishes. There were plenty of reasons for this. The company was accustomed to produce in response to orders. The industrial customers kept their own stocks, so that there was little pressure on delivery times. Because sales were becoming more unpredictable, a growing number of customers were demanding shorter delivery times. The factory's inflexible production process, involving long lead times, was not equipped for this.

The questions at the end of this step are strongly inclined towards results. There must be a clear picture of the best solution. In addition, it is extremely important to understand the level of support for the solution within the organization. In the example given, the solution has the broad support of the management and the works council. The decision on the proposal is taken immediately during the presentation meeting. Only a few more details are required, and a decision on these will be taken later.

Question 2 of the checklist mentions a *preferred solution*. Several solutions for a problem are often found. As recommended above, it is wise to report these different solutions to the principal, indicating which solutions are preferred and why.[2] The following considerations play a role here:

- Presenting several options makes it clear to the principal that the research has been carried out with a high degree of thoroughness. There are few problems for which only one solution is possible.

Table 11.1

Example of a completed logbook page for Step 8

Checklist – Step 8: Solution plan	
Questions	**Answers**
1 What solutions did you present?	• Solutions were: recruit new logistics staff (experienced logistics manager and young qualified assistant logistics manager); outsource parts of the process where there are bottlenecks; concentrate efforts on focused factory concept and take appropriate supplementary measures afterwards
2 What preferred solution did you recommend?	• First modify internal organization according to focused factory concept, then choose new logistic concept
3 Who is prepared to support this solution?	Management team and works council
4 What are the main changes for the organization?	• Dividing factory according to the product/market combinations responsible for the results • Taking on (some) new managers for the results areas
5 Who was present at the solution presentation?	• The entire management team and the works council chairman
6 What were the results of the discussion?	• Consensus on the solution • Swift implementation in view of deteriorating results
7 Who will decide about the proposals and when?	• The decision was taken during a presentation meeting. The implementation plan will be discussed in a fortnight's time at the MT meeting
8 What is the overall implementation plan?	• See item 2 – another ten days are required to flesh out the approach
9 Remarks	

■ The principal can be expected to ask for alternatives and you will be prepared for this. Presenting just one possibility can often evoke a 'take it or leave it' feeling. Managers in particular are used to thinking in terms of alternatives.

■ The principal is given the chance to prefer an option other than the one recommended, if his priorities and reasoning are different.

It is also good for students to think in terms of alternatives. This forces them to think about the quality of the recommendations and how well they can be defended.

Principals are often cautious about adopting recommendations, not so much because they distrust their quality, but because of their experience with organizational changes. They know from daily observation how much effort is involved in building up an organization and ensuring that it runs smoothly. Changes – which are usually the crux of a recommendation – almost always mean dismantling existing routines. Such activities always cost extra time and manpower, with the risk that they will not succeed.

For this reason, experienced principals will question the consultant in detail about the expected result and the feasibility of the recommendation. If the principal does follow the advice, he will wish to incorporate safeguards such as:

■ Verifying crucial assumptions and data
■ Involving the people who will be responsible for the implementation at the decision-making stage
■ Starting with a pilot implementation on a limited scale
■ Planning a phased introduction, so that adjustments can be made during each phase
■ Preparing people by means of training, etc.

A student who is aware of the way principals think and act can anticipate this. Putting forward alternatives and indicating clear evaluation criteria are suitable methods, as is contributing suggestions for safeguards such as those mentioned above. In this way a student can considerably increase the likelihood of the recommendation being accepted.

Looking again from this perspective at the recommendation for the plastics factory, we can see that a phased introduction is part of the recommendation, although at an elementary level: first convert the organization to modular factories specializing in their own market segment (focused factory concept) and then tackle the goods flow with the aim of reducing lead times. Other points, such as starting with a pilot implementation in one of the focused factories and preparing the people involved for this radical change, must be incorporated into the implementation plan.

As we have already seen during previous steps in the TSP, reporting on the activities in this step will anticipate those in the following step to a certain extent. This is necessary in order to ensure that the steps do not become targets in themselves, but remain sub-activities that have been differentiated from each other but all lead towards the final objective – achieving an effective recommendation. It is a good thing to keep the entire process in mind. However, this anticipation of the implementation within the solution plan should only be done in general terms. A good implementation plan specifies in great detail who will do what and when. That is the purpose of the implementation phase. If the report relating to the solution plan is weighed down too much with this sort of detail, the discussion of the essentials is liable to suffer. The decision-making must concentrate on the main outlines of the recommended solution. Naturally, the student must have thought through enough of the implementation to be able to answer in general terms the question, 'What does this recommendation mean for the organization?' This will give increased confidence in the recommendation.

It will be clear by now that not only is the way the recommendation has been arrived at important for its acceptance, but also the way it is communicated. Just as the feedback session is a vital aspect of the orientation phase, so the reporting of the proposed solution is a key feature of the research and solution phase.

Reporting on the solution

Firstly, the way the session is organized is important. A number of guidelines are given below, some of which are similar to what has already been said about the organization of the feedback session.

- Make sure that the people who will make the decision on the recommendation attend the meeting. This requires timely consultation with the chairman – usually the principal – on the date, place, time and duration of the meeting. It is recommended that the invitation is sent out by the chairman.
- Make sure the meeting will not be disturbed and that enough time is set aside, say one and a half to two hours.
- Consider postponing the meeting if problems arise beforehand – for example, if many people are unable to

attend or if the amount of time available is strictly limited. Consult the chairman in such cases.

- Present your report using transparencies or slides and an overhead projector or beamer and write the detailed report later, so that the results of the discussions can be incorporated.
- Keep the presentation reasonably short, so that at least half the meeting time is free for discussion and decision-making.
- Separate the presentation, including questions and explanations, from the discussion. Premature discussion can cause too much interruption and lead to the thread being lost.
- Encourage decision-making in as much detail as possible, to avoid a long wait between the recommendation and the implementation. Students can encourage prompt decision-making by pressing for firm commitments where necessary.
- Make sure that the people who will make the decisions are kept involved at intermediate stages in the consultancy process, either through working on the project or by consultation and interim reports. This means that the final recommendation will rarely hold any surprises for them. They will have followed the way the student is thinking and, if they feel happy with this, they will often make prompt decisions. The speed of decision-making is strongly influenced by the way the research and consultancy process has been organized.

An important argument for pressing for prompt decision-making is the impetus of the change process. Organizations that have been subject to and sufficiently involved in an organizational study will often anticipate the formal decisions on the recommendation. This is illustrated in Case 11.1. If too much time is taken over decisions, this can be very discouraging for the personnel involved. So at this stage of the consultancy process, it is extremely important to maintain momentum.

Case 11.1

At the plastics factory mentioned in the checklist for this chapter, the lead time is considered to be an urgent problem.

contd

Case 11.1 *contd*

In the past, the company worked without a stock of completed product. The more stringent requirements of the customers prompted it to keep a stock with a production value of 3 million. The loss of interest cancelled out the entire annual profit, so that the company found itself in the red for the first time. When the consultant set to work and started talking about 'focused factories' as the first step towards making the production process more flexible, the production managers were immediately enthusiastic. Even before the formal advisory report to the management team had been made and the decisions taken, they had set to work together to write down details of the three focused factory organizations. When the formal report was presented, it turned out that the managing director had considerable doubts about how the concept would actually work. As a result of his uncertainty the implementation was delayed by two months. This was a great disappointment to the production managers, who felt responsible for the losses being made. They had great difficulty explaining the reasons for the delay to their personnel, who had initially been extremely enthusiastic, and the commitment to the necessary reorganization gradually died down. When the director finally agreed to the implementation, after a delay of several months, he had great difficulty in getting the process started up again.

A model agenda for the meeting, which also serves as a table of contents for the report, is given below:

1   Problem statement and assignment definition
2   Summary (report only)
3   Interim results
4   Possible solutions, reasoning and preference
5   Discussion points (presentation only)
6   Discussion results (report only)
7   Global implementation plan
8   Follow-up.

We will explain some of the points mentioned in more detail.

Problem statement and assignment definition

It may seem surprising to start with the problem statement and assignment definition. After all, this component of the orientation phase was completed some time ago. But it is necessary to recap on the exact nature of the assignment to ensure that everybody is starting from the same position. If the initial agreements are not brought up again, incorrect expectations can lead to undesirable discussions.

There is another reason why it is important to start the presentation with the problem statement and assignment definition. Usually, an advisory report is drawn up after the presentation. If the subject covered is a broad one, a report of this type can have a long lifetime. It may be consulted for reference years later. If the problem statement and assignment definition on which the recommendation is based are not included in this report, this can lead to incorrect interpretation, particularly by readers who were not involved in the project. This is why merely distributing copies of the presentation slides is inadequate. These will be meaningless to uninvolved readers.

Years after the conclusion of a consultancy project, a consultant was accused of giving 'worthless' advice by a company director. Wounded pride prompted the consultant to enquire more deeply, since the recommendation had been accepted and implemented, and the company had benefited considerably from it. It turned out that the director had only seen the presentation hand-out, so that he was unaware of the missing links in the chain.

Summary

A good report starts with a 'management summary' for busy readers. This summary should only be included in the subsequent written report. It is superfluous for a slide presentation, which should be concise.

Interim results

In general, an investigation covering a fairly long period, such as a graduation fieldwork project, will include several related research activities. It is worth presenting each of these separate activities to the principal and others involved in an interim presentation.

For example, the results of a market research survey or an analysis of the production process could be presented at an early stage. As part of the final recommendation, it is advisable to briefly repeat the conclusions from these interim results, as they will not be fresh in everyone's memories.

Possible solutions, reasoning and preference

We have already described in some detail why it is best to present several solutions and to explain the reasoning that led to a preferred solution. A selection of solutions does not always present itself just like that. We would like to stress that it is advisable to force the creation of several solution options. From the in-depth research, a number of distinct options can be thought out and presented. Case 11.2 illustrates this. Presenting a wide variety of options or scenarios usually stimulates decision-making. In fact, elements of different solutions are often combined during the decision-making and implementation. By defining the individual options clearly to start with, it is easier to see how far they are being diluted. In business terms, a very distinct solution option defines a clear benchmark, which can be used to monitor the quality of the decision-making and implementation.

Case 11.2

A large company operated a computer centre for its own use, and also offered services to third parties. Judging by the sums invoiced, both externally and internally, the centre had been running at a loss for years. The non-executive board, unhappy with this situation, insisted that a consultant was called in to determine whether viable operation would ever be possible, and if so, under what conditions.

The consultant quickly realized that the main cause of the losses was the rates charged for the external work, which were far too low. The computer centre staff's lack of commercial assertiveness meant that they continuously lost out in the aggressive software market.

The consultant also noted that the parent company had followed a half-hearted policy over the years. The centre was always permitted to invest rather more than was needed for the internal requirements, for the benefit of the external work, but never enough to keep up with the external competition. The consultant decided to present a clear choice of policies in his recommendation. To this end, he drew up two alternative solutions for bringing the losses to an end:

1   Downsizing, in which the computer centre would be reduced in scale to cover only the internal demand

2   Expansion, in which substantial investment in personnel and equipment would prepare the computer centre for a profitable competitive position in the external market.

This black and white representation of the basic options prompted the non-executive board to choose option 1, thus putting an end to the half-hearted policy.

Discussion points

After the presentation of the recommendation for solving the problem, it is time for discussion. It is the chairman's task to steer the discussion in the right direction. To increase the likelihood of a good discussion, students can present a slide of discussion points. A few points that can usually be covered are:

- Initial reaction to the presentation as a whole
- The evaluation criteria used to choose the preferred solution
- Individual discussion of each solution
- Further details of the recommended solution and the global implementation plan
- Decision-making.

Presenting a number of discussion points – if possible drawn up in consultation with the chairman – will increase the impetus to make decisions during the discussion. Otherwise there is a strong chance that the limited time available for the report session will be taken up by unstructured and time-consuming discussions of sensitive but relatively unimportant details. The relevant discussion results can be included in the written report issued at a later stage, as suggested in item 6 of the table of contents.

Global implementation plan

The implementation will be examined in detail in Chapter 12. It is a good idea to anticipate this to a certain extent in the reporting session. In the discussion about the proposal, there is always the background question, 'What will have to change in our organization and in our way of working if we choose this solution?' We consider this initial discussion important, because it will show the extent to which the principal is familiar with implementing organizational changes. Our practical experience includes examples of companies where only a brief word was necessary for the implementation to be initiated. But we have also come across companies where intensive supervision was required to get the proposed organizational change under way.

A short discussion about the implementation can give you a feeling for the company's own capacity for implementation, so that you can form an opinion of the effort that will be needed to supervise it. This observation is important for specifying the activities that will be carried out in Step 9.

Follow-up

Finally, concrete agreements must be made on the follow-up activities. These may cover aspects such as:

- The definitive decision-making, especially in the unlikely event that the person who will make the final decision has not been involved at the reporting stage.
- Repeating this presentation and discussion at other meetings such as departmental meetings and management team meetings. A professional consultant may also give presentations to the works council, non-executive board or shareholders meeting. It is good practice for a student to offer to repeat the presentation where necessary. It is helpful for the principal to have the student's expertise at his disposal during each presentation. For the student, it is advantageous if the information is presented in the same format everywhere. In addition, the level of support for the recommendation in various areas of the organization will be discovered.
- Drawing up a detailed implementation plan, as covered in Step 9.

Opposition

In this phase, things are beginning to take shape. What was a long way off for many people in the organization is now becoming imminent. Something is really going to change! Some people will co-operate enthusiastically, others will now start realizing the possible consequences and will not welcome them. It is a good thing for the student to remember that for the most part opposition arises out of fear of losing status – in other words, fear of changes to responsibilities, powers or position in the formal or informal communication network.[3] This fear is sometimes justified, but misunderstandings can happen all too easily at this stage. It is extremely important for the student to communicate proactively. In other words, do not wait until you are asked to explain the plans, but try to ensure that you inform the people who are important for the project, so that they do not hear it from others. The existence of opposition is often evident from behaviour such as:

- Referring repeatedly to the disadvantages of the preferred solution
- Promoting a solution other than the preferred solution
- Remaining silent for long periods, while radiating a lack of enthusiasm and involvement
- Asking large numbers of negative questions
- Warning of the risks involved
- Subsequent attempts to meet with the consultant or student to alter his or her point of view.

We referred previously, in Step 6, to dealing with opposition and objections. The advice given then was not to exclude the people involved, but to actively include them in the research work. The same applies to making decisions about the solution and implementing it. Initiating bilateral discussions to obtain their support, including them in work groups, and using their critical attitude to hone the solution and implementation process are good ways of dealing positively with critical players.

List of action points

We conclude the discussion of this step by summing up the activities that should be carried out consecutively within it:

1   Prepare and give the advisory presentation
2   Organize the decision-making

3   Increase the level of support
4   Deal with opposition
5   Draw up the overall implementation plan
6   Complete the checklist.

Chapter notes

[1]   Schein (1999: 241) also indicates a cyclic process when he states that diagnosis and intervention take place at the same time. He argues very emphatically from a process viewpoint when he adds that every diagnostic activity also incorporates some form of intervention, and that every intervention yields new data. The distinction between these two phases is made when using models, but is purely theoretical. We are moving towards the practice of action research here. Diagnosis and intervention also alternate in action research. However, the goal is different: our approach aims at improving a situation that is perceived as a problem, while action research focuses primarily on obtaining theory that can be generalized, with organizational change being the means and by-product.

[2]   See also Kubr (2002: 217) for the importance of alternative solutions in a consultancy process.

[3]   For a detailed description of this theory, see Block (1999: 121–38).

Exercises for Step 8

11.1   Dredging company

Neox is an international manufacturer of dredgers. Its turnover is around the €400 million mark, with about 800 employees. Neox has been very successful, but its turnover and profit have stagnated recently. The managers attribute this to increasing competition, combined with the tendency of developing countries to take over part of the production of dredgers themselves to protect and boost their own industry. For Neox, this trend means that they are increasingly only receiving orders for the 'difficult' parts of dredging installations, although even these are being copied more and more.

Production takes place on the customer's order. The ships and installations are partly assembled from standard modules and partly modified to meet the specifications of the customers, the dredging companies. Most of the orders have a value of more than €5 million. The sales process is extremely long. It is not uncommon for the time spent on obtaining an order to be anything from six months to three years. The reason for this is the fact that investment goods are involved for which governments act as financiers, especially in developing countries. In addition, there is enormous overcapacity in the dredging industry. Customers take advantage of this by playing suppliers off against one another in exhausting and wasteful tender procedures.

As a consequence of these market conditions, the personnel numbers in the sales, design and cost estimation departments of Neox have increased considerably, from around 100 five years ago to the current 200. Despite this, turnover has barely improved, and the company is in danger of going into the red.

Not long ago, the commercial director, Rob Adrians, retired. The executive board had been watching the effectiveness of the commercial activities with concern for some time. Pressing Adrians for action to improve the situation had led to few results. Because of this the board decided not to appoint Adrians's deputy Gaston Leuven, but to recruit someone from outside the company. The carefully selected new commercial manager is William Catz. He is a dynamic man in his forties, a mechanical engineer by profession with extensive experience in the machinery sector, both at home and abroad.

In his previous job, his experience with fieldwork students had been very positive. He found that they are often easier to introduce into the organization than a consultancy and, with suitable supervision, they can collect and correlate a great deal of material for achieving real improvements. For this reason, Catz decided a while ago to let loose a student, Peter Barth, on the problem of the ineffective sales organization.

Peter tackled the assignment as follows. First, he familiarized himself with the market and Neox's place in it. It became clear to him that the entire dredging industry was having a difficult time. In the past all the major companies had focused their efforts on the new market segment – developing countries wishing to make their ports and waterways accessible for shipping – which led to a boom in this sector. But the tide is gradually turning. This market is becoming saturated. Customers are turning to local industrial companies, who are uninhibitedly copying the latest features from companies like Neox. Thus, only the best 'innovators' in the industry are surviving, and even then thanks only to a very sophisticated and effectively organized sales department.

Peter has completed the cycle of orientational interviews, feedback to the company, and streamlining and planning his assignment. After some discussion with the management, the assignment was eventually defined as follows:

- Increase the effectiveness of the sales organization by 50 per cent
- Develop and implement a management information system to monitor this effectiveness.

He set up a platform group so that, from time to time, he could run his ideas and findings past people who know the company well. Besides Catz, the commercial director, the platform group includes:

- Robert Cuvee, manager of the commercial cost estimation department
- Alex Ott, manager of the design department
- Harry Verwey, manager of the sales department
- Oscar Ven, manager of the information systems department.

Cuvee, Ott and Verwey report to Catz.

Peter has now reached the in-depth research stage. During the orientational interviews and the in-depth research following on from these, he has made the following observations:

- An often extremely long duration of the sales process (six months to three years)
- A limited number of orders (80–120 per year)
- The relatively high importance of each order
- A low hit rate of 15 per cent
- The very late stage at which hopeless prospects are abandoned
- The possibility of dividing the sales process into a number of separate phases.

Based on these observations, he has designed a decision model to further analyse and improve the effectiveness of the sales activities. Because the implementation of his approach involves a fairly intensive period of change, he decides to check the platform group's views of his solution plan. He therefore calls a meeting of this group to present his ideas.

1 Design the decision model for this problem.
2 Draw up the presentation Peter Barth can use to check his solution plan with the platform group.
3 Specify the three main changes that Neox will need to implement if the solution plan you have designed is accepted.

11.2 Changes as a result of outsourcing

1 What are the main organizational changes for a transport company that wishes to close down its own maintenance workshop and contract the work out to a neighbouring garage?
2 Indicate on general lines how you would implement each change.

Chapter (12)

Step 9: Implementation

In moving to Step 9, we leave behind the research and solution phase and proceed to the implementation phase of the TSP. The purpose of the research and solution phase was to carry out a thorough analysis of the causes and background of the problem under investigation, in order to produce a solution that would lead to the desired results and for which there is sufficient support within the organization. Once a solution has been chosen, the actual implementation can be initiated.

One of the basic principles of the TSP is that a fieldwork project is only successful if an organizational change takes place. In practice, the term 'organizational change' evokes a wide range of images. There will be no objections to our applying this term to major reorganization operations when thousands of people lose their jobs in a blaze of publicity. But it is less obvious to many people if we describe the introduction of a bonus system for sales reps or steps to improve the customer friendliness of telephone operators as organizational changes. Even these small-scale changes must be properly prepared, as they can easily give rise to opposition and can even result in failure. This will only become clear if you are personally involved in the implementation (see Case 12.1).

It is the practical, commonplace character of small changes that makes them so valuable to learn from. Many students will have to carry out projects of this nature in their future careers. A practical exercise during their fieldwork projects is an excellent learning experience for later life.

Case 12.1

A manager of a group of internal consultants, who until then had only carried out consultancy projects within their own company, was instructed by his superiors to transform his group into an independent external consultancy. One consequence of this was that a time registration system had to be introduced so that the hours worked could be charged to the correct customers. A work group was set up to design a suitable system incorporating time registration forms, project numbers, submission and processing procedures, computer programs for the administrative records and an invoicing system.

The design was discussed and approved and was ready to be implemented. It was then that the problems arose. Several consultants indicated that they had 'insuperable objections' to filling in time registration forms. They had suddenly realized that the time they spent on their work would become available for all to see, and that they could become accountable for this. The consultants, who had little work that could be directly charged to customers, and who spent most of their time on other useful activities, felt particularly vulnerable at this becoming so evident.

A great deal of discussion and persuasion was necessary to eliminate this sense of threat, so that the implementation could continue unhindered.

We have noticed that considerable scepticism exists among both students and supervisors over the feasibility of actually implementing the advice given in a fieldwork project. This scepticism is often based on such contentions as: there is insufficient time; it is too difficult for students; too much work is required; implementation is managers' work; or implementation requires experience. Another probable factor is that few supervisors have had direct personal experience with changing organizations. In actual fact, all supervisors are frequently involved in organizational changes without realizing it. A few examples from the life of a supervisor are:

- A new timetable
- Curriculum changes

- New rules for arranging replacement staff
- Changes to the classification of faculty subjects
- Introduction of a time registration system
- Implementation of recommendations made by supervising authorities
- Introduction of the TSP as an instrument for guiding fieldwork projects.

The definition of an organization includes task structure, staffing, systems, work forms, procedures and agreements. This means that all the examples given above come into the category of organizational changes. So even if they fail to realize it, all supervisors have considerable experience at their disposal, more than enough to instruct and support a student during this phase.

If you look at the following list of fieldwork projects from various educational establishments, the scope of the projects does not deviate drastically from what supervisors have to deal with in their own daily work:

- Setting up a central registration office
- Speeding up improvement projects
- Developing a quality measurement system
- Improving the synergy between parts of a company
- Making a support services department independent
- Choosing between in-house stock management and transport or contracting out
- Drawing up a master plan for company relocation
- Recording and improving the logistics process
- Setting up a warehouse location system.

A great deal is evidently achievable in fieldwork projects lasting four to eight months, as those above did. To reach the implementation stage, a solid project management system is necessary, along with the willingness to limit the assignment somewhat during the process. It is worth the effort.

Looking at the completed checklist (see Table 12.1), it is clear what results you should expect at the end of the activities in this step. We will deal with a number of aspects of the implementation, based on the questions and answers given in the checklist. The information in the checklist refers to the case study of the technical wholesale company TWC, which is described in detail below.

Table 12.1
Example of a completed logbook page for Step 9

Checklist – Step 9: Implementation	
Questions	**Answers**
1 What is the implementation plan?	• Announcement in Christmas speeches • Pilot project in Suffolk branch by local work group • Subsequent introduction in other branches • Internal training for branch managers
2 What is the chosen change organization?	• Management team co-ordinates and evaluates • Suffolk work group for pilot project • Work groups for other branches • Work group for branch manager training
3 What role(s) have you chosen for supporting the implementation?	• Providing support for the work groups (helper's role)
4 Which people present a risk for the implementation?	• Essex branch manager • Head office personnel manager
5 What intervention tools have been chosen to support the implementation?	• Propaganda via Christmas speech • Pilot project • Work groups of branch and head office personnel • Providing examples
6 Which consecutive 'first steps' will be carried out?	• Announcement • Pilot project
7 Remarks	

Implementation plan

The more complex organizational changes become, the more care is required in the implementation plan.[1] If the implementation plan is to be presented to the management, the following items should be specified:

- The aspects of the organization that must change to implement the chosen solution
- The substance of the change
- The people involved in the change

- The person/official who is responsible for the actual change
- The start and finish dates for the change process.

As a practical illustration, we will look at the example from the checklist in more detail. The implementation plan for the technical wholesale company TWC summarized in the checklist will be expanded and explained.

Case study: technical wholesale company TWC

The technical wholesale company TWC, with a turnover of €25 million, supplies technical tools and materials to industrial users through a head office and seven branches distributed around the country. With the appointment of a new director, discussions arose about the operating concept, revolving around the best distribution of tasks between the head office and the branches. Fundamental questions to be answered here are:

- Who purchases what in the company, and when, so that on the one hand the benefits of bulk purchasing are not lost, but on the other, the responsibility of the local branch manager for maintaining an appropriate stock level is recognized?
- Who hires the branch personnel, so that the branch manager feels responsible for the newly recruited employees while, at the same time, the head office can have confidence in the quality of the personnel?
- Who draws up the job descriptions for the branch personnel, so that their tasks fit in with the local working environment, but at the same time match up with comparable jobs elsewhere in the organization, so that a common salary system can be used and people can be easily transferred between branches, either temporarily or permanently?
- Who instructs the branch sales representatives, so that the branch manager accepts personal responsibility for the turnover, while sales efficiency and the way customers are approached are consistent from region to region?

A student was brought in to solve these problems. She observed during the feedback that the issues had both emotional and technical dimensions. The emotional aspects included the branch personnel's feeling that the head office was too paternalistic, and the head office's impression that the branches just go their own way. On a technical level, there was the question of which systems, procedures and agreements help to harmonize the separate responsibilities of the head office and the branches. A potential technical proposal is to develop a purchasing and stock management system in which the head office negotiates the master contracts in order to obtain the highest possible discount (scale benefits) but the actual orders are placed individually by each branch (stock responsibility).

Because this was a sensitive area, the student worked with a number of work groups during the in-depth research. These were deliberately composed of a few members from the head office and a few members from the branches. Each of these work groups had the task of working on one of the basic issues described. The groups worked quickly and produced satisfactory recommendations in good time. Their results included:

- An inventory of the tasks and responsibilities in each of the areas specified (purchasing/stock, personnel recruitment, job content/salary, sales instructions/approach to customers)
- The allocation of the various tasks and responsibilities to the head office, the branches or both
- The global system and procedure descriptions needed to enable the recommended working methods to operate effectively.

These recommendations were incorporated into a solution plan and reported to the management team by the student and the chairmen of the respective work groups. Because a number of members of the management team were also members of the work groups and thus shared the responsibility for the proposals, it was not difficult to obtain a favourable decision regarding their implementation.

The student now has the task of designing a detailed implementation plan. In doing this, she will take the following considerations into account:

- Each year, a Christmas speech is given in each of the organizational units (head office and branches). As the decision to introduce the new management concept was taken in November, this seems like a good opportunity for a general announcement.

■ When introducing new ways of working in an organization with a number of branches, it is better to try these out first in one branch, so that what is learned can then be used for the implementation at other branches. During the research, the manager of the Suffolk branch showed great interest and commitment to the new management concept. Therefore, Suffolk appears to be the ideal location for a pioneering role in the implementation.

■ The system and procedure descriptions are still very generalized and must be worked out in more detail. It is better for this to be done by people who will actually be working with them, as they will be familiar with the daily working procedures.

■ Not every branch manager will be sufficiently familiar with the new systems to drive them forward or take responsibility for them. In particular, the new stock management system, the new salary system (which is partly performance related), and the new way of dealing with customers on the basis of account management are new for most of the branch managers. To assist them during the implementation, an internal training course in these areas seems to be an important requirement. The best option is for this to be given after the pilot implementation, by the people who will be the first to experience the new systems and way of working, in this case those working on the pilot project in Suffolk and the head office specialists who will also participate. There are two reasons for involving head office personnel, both in developing and teaching the course and in the Suffolk pilot project. Firstly, the head office has specialists available in the relevant areas (purchasing, salaries, training, etc.), unlike the branches. Secondly, collaborating on a joint project is an ideal way of bridging the traditional 'culture gap' between head office staff and branch staff.

All these considerations led the student to an outline implementation plan, which is shown in the answers to question 1 of the checklist. The slide the student used for the presentation to the management team is shown in Table 12.2.

Table 12.2
Slide 6: TWC implementation plan

What	Who	When
1 Announcement of new management concept	• Management at head office • Branch managers at branches	During Christmas speeches
2 Pilot implementation in Suffolk branch	• Suffolk branch manager	First half of 2005
3 Details of procedures/systems	• Work group from Suffolk branch with assistance from head office	First half of 2005
4 Internal training for all branch managers	• Suffolk branch manager + head office personnel	July 2005
5 Implementation in other branches	• Work group for each branch, assisted by Suffolk and head office personnel	Second half of 2005
6 Evaluation of implementation	• Management team	6 December 2005

Change organization

When a major change in the organization is involved, it is highly likely that the change-directed activities will be neglected due to concern for the day-to-day work: 'routine drives out change'. Temporarily allocating people extra tasks as 'implementers of change' means that they will be accountable to the appropriate managers for carrying out these extra tasks. This makes it more difficult for them to use the excuse of being 'too busy with other things'. One of the jobs of the consultant or student is to suggest measures to ensure that the agreed changes are in fact implemented. With the concept 'change organization', we have in mind a coherent collection of measures of this nature.

The change organization – the second theme in the checklist – arises when large-scale changes are involved.[2] This is certainly the case for the introduction of the new management concept for the technical wholesaler TWC. The scale of an organizational change can be measured using aspects such as:

■ The number of managers and staff involved
■ The extent to which the change affects the daily work processes

- The degree to which new knowledge, understanding and skills must be acquired
- The emotional significance of the organizational change
- The time required for the change process.

Each of these criteria applies to the case described. It is therefore advisable to set up a change organization for this situation.

By a change organization, we mean a coherent collection of temporary organizational measures to make the work on the intended organizational change both visible and controllable. Temporary organizational measures are generally along the lines of *project groups, meetings, project information and training activities*. By deliberately separating these change-directed activities from the daily routine work, focus and momentum for the change process are retained.

Dealing with work groups has already been discussed in Step 6 (Chapter 9). What we described and illustrated there (Figure 9.2) about the management of the work groups applies here as well. In fact, it is often advisable to identify research work groups that were set up in Step 6 and proved to function well and assign them a role in the implementation. The knowledge they acquired during the in-depth research can be extremely valuable in the implementation phase. This does not necessarily mean that all members of the research groups will be obliged to take on an implementation task. The benefit of the accumulated knowledge still exists if even a few individual members of research work groups take part in an implementation work group.

Selecting your own role

In this chapter's checklist, the question relating to the role the student chose to support the implementation was answered with '*helper*'. Other choices of role are also possible. Table 12.3 describes a number of alternatives.[3]

As the table shows, we identify three main roles:

1   The role of *manager*. Here, the consultant leads all or part of the implementation process. In fact, he or she abandons the status of consultant and becomes interim manager or project manager.

Table 12.3
Possible roles in an implementation trajectory

Manager	Helper	Monitor
• Manages the reorganization • Takes responsibility for the result • Is given authority to take decisions • Loses distance • Gains influence and involvement • Needs a 'shadow consultant' as critical sparring partner	• Leaves management 'in charge' • Provides support in assisting role • Feels shared responsibility • Monitors progress and results • Keeps a distance, stands apart from the parties involved	• Has a position in the steering committee • Gives advice if problems arise • Is critical observer • Alerts management to any deviation from the chosen course

The characteristics of this role are given in Table 12.3 and are self-evident. A consultant who takes on this role must have proven management qualities in order to carry out the implementation successfully. Not all consultants have these qualities. Many consultants are very competent in providing directions to reach the solution without actually being good managers. A good football coach is certainly not always a former top football player.

When a consultant takes on the role of manager, it is important that he or she is backed up by a shadow consultant, to help monitor the prescribed course. During the implementation, all sorts of unexpected developments or situations can arise that demand compromises. A fellow consultant, who is free from these influences, can help monitor the dividing line between what is essential and what is possible during such changes of direction.

For students, we strongly advise against taking on a management role in a large-scale change process – for example, as the chairman of a steering committee. Lack of experience increases the risks for both the student and the company.

2   The role of *helper*. This is far more manageable for students. For example, by taking on the role of secretary of all or the most important work groups, a student can exert considerable influence on the operation of these groups and can be of assistance without having to tackle

the toughest problems himself or herself. Helping should not mean that the company personnel take a back seat. Occasionally, a work group will sit back and watch an over-assiduous student carry out the task. It is not difficult to imagine the consequences. Once the student's project is finished, everything will break down. Professional consultants know this and have learned to assist where necessary without becoming involved in matters that the company is tackling itself. It is not difficult for them to play this role. Their high fees usually impose an extremely selective level of commitment.

3   The role of *monitor*. This is often chosen by professional consultants. In this role, they play the part of the shadow consultant, or you might say they are the 'conscience' of the company management responsible for the implementation as a whole. The main activities of a consultant in this role may be as a member of the steering committee or a temporary participant in any management team meetings where the change operation is being discussed. The consultant–monitor takes no part in the implementation activities as such, which means he or she can keep a critical eye on any changes to the approach.

This is not an ideal role for a student either. Although it presents fewer problems than the management role, it still requires talents that the student will only possess to a limited degree. The main demand made of a person in this role is to assess accurately and in good time what risks are involved in changing the approach, and to be able to communicate this opinion to the management with authority and conviction. In addition, this role requires a level of continuity that does not fit in with the limited duration of a fieldwork project.

In practice, the roles described above can be mixed. In some cases, the consultant–manager or consultant–monitor can also play the role of consultant–helper.

In general, these mixed roles are inadvisable. For people in an organization, frequent changes of role by an external consultant are extremely confusing. When people are interviewed by a consultant, most of them respond with an openness which they could regret if this same consultant were to become their supervisor or fellow manager soon afterwards. People can easily feel deceived and imposed upon, and this is very detrimental to the consultant's activities and to the image of the profession.

Risk factors

Question 4 in the checklist for Step 9 is aimed at identifying any opposition to the solution to be implemented. In almost every consultancy process and for every solution, opposition will arise, as we have already mentioned on several occasions. Once a solution has been chosen and is to be implemented, the opponents are expected to co-operate loyally in implementing the chosen solution. By then, it is clear that there is ample support for this solution within the organization. In general, opponents do co-operate, but experienced consultants know that they can find the implementation particularly difficult. They must commit themselves to a different way of working, while they are not convinced that this change will be an improvement. This is hard for some people. The natural tendency is to involve these opponents only marginally or not at all in the change process. We have already argued that a more satisfactory end result is obtained if these people are in fact intensively involved. Welcoming them on board, making them members of a work group and giving them responsibility for part of a project are ways of putting their critical attitude to positive use. In practice, their resistance often decreases and is sometimes even transformed into enthusiasm. To encourage this, it is a good thing for the student or consultant to pay them special attention – for example, with an extra personal meeting or additional support. This also reduces the risk that opponents may focus more, often unconsciously, on proving that the chosen solution is inappropriate than on contributing to an effective implementation.

Intervention tools

Question 5 of the checklist is concerned with intervention tools. An intervention tool is a measure or a number of linked measures that the consultant can suggest to the management to support an organizational change. A great deal has been written about interventions and intervention methods, and many methods have appeared on the market, varying from simple to extremely complicated interventions.[4] We will limit ourselves here to a number of forms of intervention that are within the scope of the student.

Our starting point is that the organizational change itself is managers' work. But a student can certainly contribute, on the basis of the 'tool-kit' illustrated, by making useful intervention proposals and by offering assistance.

Communication

The intended change is widely communicated by means of announcements, personnel publications, noticeboards, meetings, etc. This can be a powerful instrument. A director once announced in a Christmas speech that he would be paying extra attention to the high levels of absence from work. The absence level promptly fell by 20 per cent.

Pilot project

A pilot project is often chosen if there are complex changes to be made. The real difficulties involved in changing an organization – for example, a new production planning method in the factory – will only become apparent during the actual implementation. To prevent these initial problems from bringing the entire plant to a standstill, it is better to start by gaining experience in one small section. This limits the risks and results in a better approach to introducing the new planning system in the other sections. It also means that personnel from the pilot section can help their colleagues in the other sections with the experience they have gained.

Management instruction

The people involved are informed in writing how the new way of working is to be introduced and from when. This is an effective method for small, simple changes that are not particularly sensitive. An example is a request from the directors of a consultancy to the consultants not to leave customer dossiers on their desks in future, in view of the confidential nature of the information and the fact that some dossiers have gone missing.

Training

Training is a frequently used and very effective aid in generating new understanding and skills that are needed for an organizational change. An example is a marketing course for the field personnel of a company's health and safety office, which is being made independent and will be looking for customers in the external market.

Feedback

Giving feedback means informing a person or a group in objective terms how their work is regarded through the eyes of an outsider. The description can be based on observations made by the person giving the feedback or on observations collected from other people.

Examples of both types are:

- From personal observation – 'I do not see you often at meetings or in the canteen. This gives me the impression that you do not feel much involvement with this organization.'
- From the observations of others – 'The customer survey indicates that our company is not regarded as very service orientated.'

Giving feedback is a way of improving people's understanding of the way they work, with the objective of increasing their willingness to co-operate with the intended changes.

Setting examples

People or groups who have mastered the new way of working can be held up as an example to others to encourage them to join in too. One possibility is to ask them to give a presentation during a regular work meeting.

Rewards and punishments

By praising and rewarding the desired developments and rejecting or penalizing undesirable developments, personnel are encouraged to pick up the organizational change quickly. The 'rewards and punishments' must be translated into organizational measures, such as:

- Rewards – a complimentary remark, being held up as an example, a bonus, a good appraisal result, a higher pay rise, promotion.
- Punishments – a critical remark, no bonus, no promotion, poor appraisal result, no pay rise.

A consultant who takes a positive view may suggest only rewards to his principal, as not receiving these rewards is often 'punishment' enough to prompt others to make more effort to support the intended organizational change.

Replacing or relocating staff

Replacement or relocation is used to reinforce the change-directed approach to an organization or part of it. If there are doubts about the capability of a key figure in the process – for example, the manager of a department that is important in the change process – to achieve the intended change in his group, someone else may be put in charge of the group, temporarily or otherwise (see Case 12.2).

Case 12.2

The turnover of an engineering bureau was too low, and a consultant advised it to change the organization of its sales approach. However, the present sales manager was regarded as totally unsuitable for the new approach. So a replacement with better marketing skills was recruited internally and the sales manager went back to more technical tasks.

'Small steps' forward

The reasoning behind question 6 in the checklist is our stance that, in general, organizational changes can best be implemented in small steps that generate quick success. Small steps are easier to keep track of, easier to adapt if something seems likely to go wrong, they can be carried out faster and, if they proceed smoothly, they set the trend for the rest of the change process. In addition, these small, quick successes will help the sceptics – and there are always sceptics – to overcome their doubts. 'Small steps' may be:

- One pilot department
- One stand-alone section of a much more extensive procedural change
- One pilot market in the region
- Several pilot customers
- One item from the product range (or a group of items)
- One branch
- One layer in the organization – for example, for the implementation of a new appraisal system
- One intervention tool to see what the effect is.

Organizational changes initiated in this way generally proceed much more effectively than all-embracing changes carried out all together, with extensive schedules, etc. One requirement, though, is that there must be enough time to work through the change step by step. If this is a crisis situation – for example, to prevent an imminent bankruptcy – the time is often unavailable, and the management is forced to take major risks.

We hope it is now clear that students can definitely participate in implementation activities and that this phase is often an extremely valuable part of the fieldwork project. To further support the activities of students in this area, we make a number of practical suggestions. Some of them have already been covered briefly earlier in this book.

Suggestions

Allow others to take responsibility

As far as possible, pass any supervisory roles to the people responsible and make motions of withdrawal. The organization will have to continue without you when you leave. This will require a certain amount of self-control, as there is often a strong tendency to remain in the limelight.

Motivation is more important than rules

The success of an organizational change is determined more by what people are able and willing to do than by rules and guidelines, such as task descriptions, organizational charts and working instructions. These elements can reinforce people's 'ability and willingness' but they will seldom generate it from scratch.

Not every manager is a change manager

Not all managers who can control an operational organization are equally good at managing change processes. If it turns out that a manager lacks this quality, temporary help from an interim manager can provide a good and socially responsible solution.

Make it possible to discuss personal failure

Following on from what we said above, it is important to have the courage to enable the discussion of personal failure. Organizational changes are times when previously capable people find themselves in a new role for which they are not suited. For example, a sales representative who achieved excellent results by visiting customers personally may prove hopelessly inadequate in a transition to a telephone sales approach. This problem is often ignored until real damage is done. However, a consultant or even a student monitoring the process can break the taboo in their role as helper. By discussing the problem with the person concerned and the manager responsible, unfortunate developments can be prevented and a satisfactory solution can often be reached. Make sure you talk to the person concerned first and then take further action together.

Company interests take priority over individual interests

If difficult choices have to be made, the interests of the company must take priority over the interests of individual employees. A change process that is important for the company must be implemented in the interests of all those who work in or are connected with the company, even when personal interests suffer.

Naturally, everything within reason should be done to alleviate the individual 'pain'.

List of action points

Once again, we conclude this step in the TSP by summarizing the actions that must be carried out successively:

1   Draw up and present the detailed implementation plan
2   Choose role(s)
3   Choose intervention methods
4   Set up change organization
5   Increase the level of support
6   Encourage management supervision
7   Make motions of withdrawal
8   Complete the checklist.

Chapter notes

[1] The importance of an implementation plan is stressed by Greiner and Metzger (1983: 269) when they observe that the weakest point of experienced consultants is generally the implementation phase:

> It is amusing but sad to find so many consultants who assume that change occurs automatically once a lengthy and lucid report is presented that lays out a list of recommendations. This superficial approach is reminiscent of expecting a customer to buy a new car based on an impersonal letter from an unknown car dealer.

Schaffer (2002: 8–9) formulates the basic principle that a 'high impact consultant' works explicitly to strengthen the skills the customer will need to implement the proposal.

[2] Parallels with what we mean by 'change organization' can be found in Kubr (2002: 215 onwards), who makes various suggestions for working specifically on the implementation of proposals.
A fundamental discussion of the backgrounds to change processes in organizations can be found in Katz and Kahn (1978: 653).

[3] See Chapter 9, note 4.

[4] One source describing intervention strategies is Harvey and Brown (2005).

Exercises for Step 9

Coffee Machines Ltd

Joe Klinkenberg, director of a company selling coffee vending machines, has invited a student to investigate a number of issues within his company. Klinkenberg first entered the vending machine business when he was offered the agency for an Italian coffee machine in this country. As a former canteen manager, he had some awareness of the prospects in this market and this is how he came to start up his own company.

The step was a profitable one for him. He has now achieved an annual turnover of about 10 million, with a very acceptable profit. But in his opinion changes are inevitable. The Italian coffee machine manufacturer is constantly bombarding him with new models: higher capacity, better coffee, combinations with other hot drinks, etc. Klinkenberg has always loyally incorporated the new options into his sales dossier and sent his representatives off to customers with the products. But this has gradually developed into an extensive range that no longer suits all customers.

The representatives themselves have also developed a certain degree of specialization. Some tend to look for contacts among small and medium-sized businesses, where vending machines are installed in offices and factories. Others do better in the sports and leisure sector (camp-sites, amusement arcades, sports club bars), where it is important that the machines cannot be broken into easily. The advertising campaigns and mailings for the various target groups have also become specialized.

All in all, Klinkenberg had good reasons for inviting a student to investigate the commercial policy of Coffee Machines Ltd for the coming years. The student tackled the research energetically, after some initial discussions about the definition of the assignment, the setting up of a platform group, etc. Surveys of the market and of the competition were carried out, the product range was examined, and interviews were held with the sales personnel and other people closely involved.

The student made regular interim reports and presented his final recommendation a few weeks ago. This recommendation indicates that the market is becoming differentiated into a number of segments, with different requirements for equipment, sales approach and service. For Coffee Machines Ltd, this means that differentiation must also be made in the internal organization in order to best serve each of the different segments.

The student's proposals include:

- Setting up separate sales groups for each market segment
- Recording turnover and results for each sales group
- Holding separate advertising campaigns for each market segment and monitoring their impact.

In summary, this means far-reaching changes in the organizational structure, the tasks of the sales managers and sales staff, and the administration system.

Klinkenberg and his staff accept the student's ideas. But now that the actual implementation is imminent, nobody knows exactly how to go about it. They have therefore asked the student – who still has time for this – to help with the implementation.

1 Draw the organization diagram for the new sales organization.
2 Prepare a presentation of the detailed implementation plan and the change organization you propose.
3 Which three intervention methods would you recommend with priority to support the implementation of the new sales organization and why?
4 Which choice of role would you recommend for the student and why?

Effectiveness of instruction and training

Instruction and training are important intervention methods to help people cope with new or changed methods of working. A frequent problem, however, is that what is learnt is not put into practice.

What steps can be taken to encourage new knowledge to be used in practice, split into:

- Steps that form part of the instruction/training
- Steps that follow on from the instruction/training.

Chapter (13)

Step 10: Conclusion and evaluation

When a consultancy project is nearing its end, a professional consultant will carry out a number of concluding activities.[1] Students too must finalize their project in a satisfactory manner. The activities for concluding the assignment are as follows:

- Draw up a final report
- Hold a number of concluding interviews
- Ask the principal for an evaluation of the project
- Take your leave.

To start with, we will use the completed checklist for this chapter (Table 13.1) to give an example of these concluding activities. The questions asked in the checklist will be used as a basis for discussing the concluding activities. The answers to the checklist questions are taken from a fieldwork project for an industrial insurance board. The student developed an information system that can and must be consulted by the insurance board personnel at various locations before they start work on developing a new 'information tool'. They must consult the new system beforehand to find out whether someone else in the organization has already solved their particular problem. It was clear that if the amount of duplicated work done in the past could be reduced, considerable savings could be made.

The main theme of the checklist is that the student looks back critically at the project, together with the principal and the other people who have played an important role in the project. This means evaluating the way people worked together, whether the results meet expectations, whether there were times or situations when the project did not proceed in the way that had been

Table 13.1
Example of a completed logbook page for Step 10

Checklist – Step 10: Conclusion and evaluation	
Questions	**Answers**

1 Has a final report been presented within the company? If so, what were the results?	• Yes. Results were:
	  – Contribution was regarded as positive
	  – Request to stay and help with implementation for two months after graduation
	  – Prospect of a job after that!

2 With which people did you hold concluding interviews?	• With the executive board, management team, works council chairman and non-executive board chairman
3 What did you learn from the project evaluation?	• Some doubts existed during the early months • After that, systematic approach and commitment were valued • Presentations could be improved
4 Who did you discuss the project evaluation with?	• With the director and deputy director (= company coach) • With the fieldwork supervisor
5 What arrangements have been made for you to take your leave of the company?	• Coffee and cake on Friday afternoon
6 What is your own evaluation and what points for improvement do you see for yourself?	• I learned a lot, not easy to work in accordance with the TSP, but customer noticed the effect! • Points for improvement: monitor planning better and improve presentations
7 Remarks	

hoped or desired, what causes this could be attributed to, etc. The main question for the student, and also for the company, is naturally, 'What can we learn from these experiences for future projects'?

Final report

Various interim reports were produced in the course of the project, initially as a slide presentation, followed up by a written version. We recommend using the same twofold approach for the final report, but with a few differences:

- An implementation report, describing the status of the implementation and any recommendations for finishing off the change process after your departure. This report also serves as an interim report, since your departure is a milestone in an organizational change that will be completed in the future. The recommended format for this is a presentation to the management team followed by a written report.
- The final report on the entire consultancy process, explaining the work done by the student, for the benefit of the principal and the educational supervisors.

The final report for the educational establishment must be a comprehensive written report.

The same type of report is also valuable for the principal for reference purposes and as a source of information for those who were only involved in the project from a distance, such as non-executive directors, shareholders or bankers.

Fieldwork supervisors sometimes impose conditions for a final report that make it less useful for the company where the fieldwork project took place. Examples of this are insisting on an extensive discussion of the literature or an exhaustive explanation of research models used. Our experience shows that the requirements of both parties can be satisfied by a single report if both sets of interests are kept in mind. As an aid to this, we have developed the following standard layout for a fieldwork report.

Example 13.1: Standard layout for a fieldwork report

1.	Table of contents	1	
2.	Summary	2	
3.	Introduction and problem definition	2	(Steps 1 and 2)
4.	Description of company/external developments	5	(Steps 3 and 4)
5.	Assignment formulation	2	(Step 5)
6.	Plan of action	5	(Step 6, including literature review and working model)
7.	Execution of assignment	15	(Step 7)
8.	Summary, conclusions and recommendations	3	(Step 8)
9.	Implementation	10	(Step 9)
10.	Evaluation of project	5	(Step 10)
Total		50 pages	

A final report drawn up along these lines satisfies the following requirements:

- The layout fits in with the TSP working method described in this book. The checklist questions and the action points that conclude each step act as guidelines. Smart students will prepare a dossier at the beginning of the project in which they file the documentation for each step (reading material, research results, interview notes, interim reports, etc.). This provides an organized and accessible starting point for writing the final report. Interim reports can often be incorporated into the final report, with some modification if necessary.

- Reports drawn up in accordance with the proposed layout will provide principals with what they expect from a good consultancy report – a 'management summary' (Chapter 2), the assignment formulation (Chapter 5), plan of action (Chapter 6) and the final recommendation (Chapter 8). The size of the report is also acceptable (no more than 50 pages). Lengthy details can be recorded in appendices.

- This layout satisfies the course requirements – it contains information making it possible for the student to be assessed on how the TSP has been followed, the methodical justification (Chapter 7), the theoretical reasoning and literature review (Chapter 7), and the evaluation of the assignment (Chapter 10).

Producing a single report that satisfies both the company and the fieldwork supervisor also makes it possible to assess whether the student has picked up the 'company jargon' satisfactorily. This ability will be important in his or her future career.

Concluding interviews and evaluation of assignment

The main purpose of the concluding interviews is to take your leave of the company in an organized manner. The interviews also provide an ideal opportunity to assess the level of customer satisfaction and to learn from the work carried out.

For professional consultants, another function of these interviews is to keep the door open for future assignments. Reviewing the results achieved from the partnership can confirm the principal's view that the consultant or consultancy would be the right choice for a future project. The consultant has the advantage of knowing the company already, so that little time will be required to learn about its operation on a subsequent occasion.

This commercial aspect may also be relevant for students. In practice, students are frequently offered a temporary or permanent job after the fieldwork project. In any event, it is sensible to be aware of this possibility and to explicitly raise the subject of jobs.

If the project has gone well, students can almost always obtain a favourable reference, which can be used when applying for a job with another company. The student should request this.

The concluding interviews are held with people who have been sufficiently involved in the consultancy project that they can be expected to have an opinion about the performance of the consultant or student.

For a student, these will generally be:

- The principal
- The company coach
- The chairman and members of the management team
- Chairmen of work groups
- Personnel in the working area involved
- The chairman of the works council.

To give substance to the interviews, some preparatory work is advisable. This can include the following activities:

- Design an evaluation form appropriate for the assignment and the fieldwork company, highlighting the most important measurable features for evaluating the quality of the consultancy work. As a pointer, the evaluation form used by one consultancy is shown in Figure 13.1.
- After giving verbal notification in advance, present this evaluation form to all the people with whom you wish to hold a concluding interview. Ask them to fill in the form and send it back well before the interview.
- Make a complete inventory of the answers received and use this as part of your final report. Use the forms filled in by the individual respondents during the concluding interviews, and make a note of the learning points raised.

Holding effective concluding interviews is an art that certainly requires practice. The most difficult thing is to listen to negative

Name: ....

Organization: ....

Date: ....

Our questions are divided into a number of categories:
- Lighthouse as a consultancy
- the Lighthouse consultants
- the project result
- overall impression

You can give your opinion on a scale of 1 to 10. Please fill in this form as completely as possible. If there are aspects you consider important that are not included on the form, please mention these in your answer to question 16.

	Open to much improvement	Moderate	Excellent	No opinion

Lighthouse as a consultancy

1. The reaction of the Lighthouse organization to questions and problems was — 1 [ ][ ][ ] 5 [ ][ ][ ] 10 — [ ]
2. The clarity of the proposed project/contract was — 1 [ ][ ][ ] 5 [ ][ ][ ] 10 — [ ]
3. The Lighthouse presentation in correspondence, quotation, reports and invoices was — 1 [ ][ ][ ] 5 [ ][ ][ ] 10 — [ ]

The lighthouse consultants

4. The reaction of the Lighthouse consultants to questions and problems was — 1 [ ][ ][ ] 5 [ ][ ][ ] 10 — [ ]
5. The ability of the consultant(s) to express themselves
   a. in writing was — 1 [ ][ ][ ] 5 [ ][ ][ ] 10 — [ ]
   b. verbally was — 1 [ ][ ][ ] 5 [ ][ ][ ] 10 — [ ]
6. The contact between the consultant(s) and your organization and its members was — 1 [ ][ ][ ] 5 [ ][ ][ ] 10
7. The ability of the consultant(s) to empathize with the problems, working methods and culture of your organization was — 1 [ ][ ][ ] 5 [ ][ ][ ] 10 — [ ]
8. The expertise of the consultant(s) in your problem area was — 1 [ ][ ][ ] 5 [ ][ ][ ] 10 — [ ]

The project result

9. The interim information given on the progress of the project and the results was — 1 [ ][ ][ ] 5 [ ][ ][ ] 10 — [ ]
10. The interim information given on the running time and cost was — 1 [ ][ ][ ] 5 [ ][ ][ ] 10 — [ ]
11. The final running time of the project was — 1 [ ][ ][ ] 5 [ ][ ][ ] 10 — [ ]
12. The usefulness of the final recommendation was — 1 [ ][ ][ ] 5 [ ][ ][ ] 10 — [ ]

Overall impression

13. Please circle the three points from 1-12 where Lighthouse can improve the most.

14. Would you consider calling in Lighthouse for a future project?

	No	Definitely	No opinion
	1 [ ][ ][ ] 5 [ ][ ][ ] 10		[ ]

15. If you have experience with other consultancies: which ones are these and how does Lighthouse score in comparison?
16. General verdict, with comments and additions.

Thank you for your co-operation.

Figure 13.1
Example of an evaluation form for a consultancy.

points of your work being described without interrupting or becoming defensive. This is even harder if you consider that these are inaccurate or were perhaps even caused by the respondent. There are people who cannot help exploding in such situations, leading to the failure of the interview. Remember, the purpose of the evaluation is to look back with an open mind at each person's perception of the partnership, so that both sides can learn from it.

Angry words will destroy any receptiveness and break down the learning process.

A few guidelines for successful evaluation are given below:

- Explain the purpose of the interview very clearly and show that you are looking for points that you can learn from and improve on, and that there is no question of assigning blame.
- Take the process as the main theme of the interview and go through it with the respondent. Ask their opinion about each significant event.
- Record their comments. Ask further questions at points where criticism is given, as these generally yield the most material for learning and improvement.
- Even if aggressive criticism is made, remain neutral and ask for further details, observing and recording in an objective manner.
- After the process analysis, recap on the points of criticism and ask for advice on how you could handle these aspects better another time. You can certainly query whether changes in the way the respondent acted might also have facilitated or improved the interaction. After all, evaluation involves analysing the process to identify points that can be improved upon, and these points could involve either party.
- Finally, sum up the points for learning and improvement, and extend your thanks for the useful discussion.

This is a difficult undertaking for some students, prompting them to steer well clear of concluding interviews or, at the very least, to approach only those people with a favourable attitude. This is a pity as far as the learning process is concerned, as they miss a unique chance to master something that will permeate their entire professional life. It is more courageous to at least make an attempt. If you lack confidence, ask your fieldwork supervisor to allow you to practise with him or her.

Your own evaluation

The student's own learning points that were noted in the checklist form an important part of the conclusion of the fieldwork project. The fieldwork project is usually the first time that students come face to face with the interesting reality of how an organization operates over a significant period of time. They learn that skills and knowledge, theory and practice must be combined together to achieve success. You must have a thorough theoretical understanding of your subject. But you must also develop social discipline and interaction skills – keeping to agreements, taking responsibility for tangible results, finding innovative solutions to awkward problems, improvisation, making and maintaining contacts, taking part in forthright discussions, translating criticism into learning points.

Our educational system puts little emphasis on social discipline and interaction skills, which is why fieldwork is so essential. The TSP has been created to rise to the challenge of working in practical situations. It is better to become familiar with the difficulties during this final stage in your education, and make mistakes now and again, while this is still acceptable, rather than to leave all the mistakes to be made during your first job.

Chapter note

[1] Kelly (1986: 232) gives concrete suggestions for evaluating the consultant's own performance.

Lippitt and Lippitt (1994: 126) describe a model for evaluating a consultancy process. Hale (1998: 179) gives a list with 'key measures, criteria to measure, metrics'.

Exercises for Step 10

13.1   Evaluation of effects

■ Design the questionnaire for the student's final evaluation at Coffee Machines Ltd (Exercise 12.1).

■ What conceivable observations at Coffee Machines Ltd could lead you to assume that the proposed organizational change will be continued, even after the student has left?

■ Which people at Neox (Exercise 11.1) should Peter Barth definitely hold an evaluation interview with before leaving?

13.2   Coping with critical feedback

During the evaluation of his fieldwork project, a student was subjected to considerable criticism:

- Too much time spent on the orientation phase, which in the principal's opinion was avoiding the real work
- Playing personnel off against each other by confronting them with each other's opinions, which varied considerably, during the interviews
- Working with work groups that produced no results, instead of getting on with the work himself
- A vague and useless report
- Unnecessary and time-consuming presentations to the management team about all sorts of issues that were already known and/or unimportant
- In general, far too little knowledge of the sector and the products that are important to the company.

In other words, the fieldwork project was a failure and there was no positive feedback to the educational establishment.

1   For each of the criticisms made, indicate how this might have been prevented.
2   How would you act if you received negative criticism of this nature as a student?
3   What conditions should your company coach satisfy to help prevent a situation like this occurring?
4   How would you react to a request to return to the company on a 12-month contract after your (imminent) graduation in order to make the fieldwork project a success?

Part 3

Divergent scenarios

Introduction to Part 3

In this book the Ten-Step Plan is presented as a guide to carrying out effective student fieldwork projects. It is derived from organizational consultancy practice and can also be used as a working framework in that context. Like all models, however, this template of the organizational consultancy process is a subset of the varied reality on which it is based.

The top priority for students is the success of their own fieldwork project, but those who wish to continue in the exciting profession of organizational consultancy will experience the limitations of this approach. There are consultancy situations in which the TSP model cannot be followed as it stands, and it must be possible to deviate from the plan made.

In this section, we discuss a number of situations that frequently arise in consultancy practice that cannot be dealt with by rigidly following the TSP model. The variations described here are all fundamentally linked to the relationship between the consultant and the principal. The TSP was designed to suit a fieldwork project situation, with the following characteristics:

- The issue involved is relevant to the company, but rarely so critical that the continued existence of the company is at stake.
- The company normally makes an agreement with the student and/or the educational establishment to pay a specified, generally modest, remuneration for the period in which the student is working on the project.
- Students are generally given the freedom to develop their own solutions. One common reason for bringing in a student is that the company welcomes the input of up-to-date specialist knowledge.
- The company provides a coach for the student. This company coach generally exercises considerable influence on the project.

In many cases, the situation in which a professional consultant works does not match this profile. They are more often called in when problems are urgent and must be solved quickly. A standard approach is sometimes necessary.

This section starts off by describing the profile of the principal in the TSP approach. It then shows how an alternative approach is sometimes required in practice. Alternatives are mentioned only briefly.

Even if there are good reasons for deviating from the TSP when designing a consultancy process, it is usually possible to follow the main principles of the TSP. Support, involvement, focus on results, harmonization with external developments and a manageable project approach are the foundations of every effective consultancy process.

Chapter 14

Alternative consultancy processes

Up to now, this book has consisted of a description of the Ten-Step Plan and its application to the specific circumstances of students faced with the task of carrying out an effective fieldwork project. The starting point was that the fieldwork project could be regarded as a consultancy project and that students can apply the principles of organizational consultancy work to achieve success in their fieldwork projects. This focus on the fieldwork project unavoidably brings a degree of simplification to the real-life situation from which the TSP was developed. Anyone using the TSP in practice for organizational consultancy work will need to be familiar with many other variations and be able to cope with alternatives.

In our view, what has been written so far is sufficient for carrying out a fieldwork project successfully. The immediate introduction of all the variations and alternatives that occur in practice would only cause confusion for students who still have to learn to maintain the course of a project. Students who have little experience of real-life work situations need instructive guidelines that are not excessively complex. Questions about other, possibly better, ways of working are best left for a later date.

However, in our view, the simplification of reality presented in this book requires some further explanation. This simplification may unintentionally lead to a degree of dogmatism. We will therefore conclude this manual by adding a brief summary of possible variations and alternatives. This does not change the fact that it is desirable to follow the TSP closely for fieldwork projects. However, for your future professional career it is useful to have some knowledge of other routes that can be followed.

In this chapter, we will first look at the assumptions made about the assignment and the customer/principal on which the TSP is based. Variations on these assumptions will then be examined. This offers the opportunity to describe the corresponding alternative consultancy processes at the same time. Unlike the preceding chapters, this section will not focus primarily on the role of the student, but will be geared towards the work of professional consultants dealing with principals who are acting on the basis of commercial considerations.

Profile of the customer in the TSP approach

The way a consultant approaches a specific consultancy process is determined to a great extent by the consultant's understanding of the needs of the customer for whom the consultancy process is intended. Some principals are in a great hurry and need a consultant to start quickly and continue the work rapidly. In other cases, a principal is primarily looking for a consultant with authority, because additional powers of persuasion are needed in the company's specific situation. Another possibility is where principals have their own clear preference for a particular way of dealing with the problem and are looking for a consultant from that perspective.

Consultants alway need to deal with such customer-specific situations. Obviously, they can modify their own approach somewhat if they can be convinced of the importance of this, but there are limits. If the principal requires a quick scan and the consultant cannot complete the project within six months, then they have a problem.

If we take another look at the TSP approach with this in mind, we see that the TSP works on the basis of a specific customer situation:

- The assignment is not of an urgent nature
- The principal is not requesting competitive tenders from different consultants
- The principal values customized work
- The principal also requires supervision of the implementation
- The principal and consultant decide on the working programme together.

We will briefly cover each of these assumptions, with a description of alternative consultancy situations.

The assignment is not of an urgent nature

In the TSP, a relatively long time is spent on preparations for actually carrying out the assignment. This is a deliberate investment that makes it possible to appraise and streamline the project. It also involves activities that generate support for the change process.

However, situations occur in practice in which the principal has more need of a quick response and recommendation than thoroughness and gaining support. This happens primarily in the case of highly threatening business developments. If the position of a company is so bad that bankruptcy is feared, recommendations aimed at preventing the disaster become extremely urgent. This applies, for example, to a 'perspective study' carried out on the instructions of a bank. The central task is to find out whether the company has any chance of survival and, if so, what intervention is necessary to achieve it. In this case, the bank will make the continuation of credit dependent on the results of the study. If sufficient prospects for continuation are identified, financing will be made available for the reorganization, which usually involves radical cutbacks. On the other hand, if a survival strategy has little prospect of success, the credit will be terminated and the company is almost certainly past redemption.

In this perspective study, consultants must immediately focus their attention on the aspects most crucial for survival. These aspects primarily include the opportunities in the market, the commercial assertiveness, the possibilities for extensive cost reduction by reducing personnel numbers and selling off unnecessary equipment, and the restoration of viable business operation by means of outsourcing activities more cheaply, collaboration or complete integration with a financially strong partner.

In fact, in a consultancy situation like this, the role of the principal is no longer taken by the company management but by the bank responsible for the financing. If the chances of survival are initially deemed to be small, experienced consultants will often request a bank guarantee to cover all or part of their invoice, to make sure that they are not left with an irrecoverable debt as a result of the company's collapse.

Urgent assignments are not only prompted by acute business continuity problems. Other circumstances can also force managers into tight situations requiring a rapid recommendation from a consultant. This can frequently be attributed to delays in internal decision-making. For a wide variety of reasons, external help before a proposed decision is taken can become urgent. The timing of the decision is fixed and it has taken too long to realize that external help would be useful or necessary. We give a few examples from our own consultancy experience (see Case 14.1).

Case 14.1

- A European subsidiary of an American multinational suddenly hears that the vice-president is coming over from America in a fortnight's time to evaluate the strategic plan. In view of the inevitability of this visit and the fact that no such plan exists, a consultant is hastily found to help 'save face' and 'put together a strategic plan'.
- A sales director has decided with his sales staff to hold a two-day workshop to draw up the sales plan for the following year. However, during the preparations it becomes evident that there is so much tension within the group that he decides the week before the workshop to call in the assistance of an external consultant during the workshop.
- Three companies decide to set up a joint project with the assistance of an external consultant. One of the directors undertakes to look for a suitable consultant for this purpose. However, he fails to do this because of a lack of time. He realizes his error a week before the date set for the start of the project, and then has to find someone in a hurry who can start the research activities the following week.

'Last-minute' assignments like these differ from consultancy projects revolving round imminent disaster. The room to manoeuvre is not limited by the bank in this case, but by a commitment that has been made. Managers do not always realize the importance of a well-prepared consultancy process, so they sometimes attach more value to meeting an internal commitment than to a good starting position for the consultant.

An experienced consultant learns to cope with this type of consultancy process without letting it adversely affect the quality of his or her work. One way of doing this is to separate the urgent parts of the work from the less urgent, thereby achieving acceptable time scales for the total process. Another option is to reduce the pressure of the internal commitment by convincing the customer that, although it is possible to work quickly, the likelihood of actually achieving useful results in this way is very small.

The principal is requesting competitive tenders from different consultants

Consultancy work can involve substantial costs for the customer. Consultancy assignments worth hundreds of thousands of euros are not unusual, even for medium-sized companies. This sometimes encourages potential customers to invite several consultancies to tender for a specific job. Smart negotiation can often lead to a sizeable reduction in consultancy expenditure.

However, if every tendering consultancy were to carry out Steps 1–5 of the TSP in order to reach a clear assignment definition, plan of action and corresponding budget, this would lead to an impractical situation. For example, no customer would be prepared to allow several consultants who have not yet been selected to each hold a number of orientational interviews. This would be an unacceptable burden on the organization.

The TSP as described in this book assumes that a consultant has been chosen by the principal and is given the opportunity to carry out an orientation phase before the final contract is drawn up. This professional orientation phase – also called preliminary research – need not last more than a few days.

So how does a consultancy process work when there is an element of competition involved? The company usually provides the tendering consultancies with the same information about the company and the intended assignment, either verbally, in writing or a combination of both. Using this information, the consultants draw up a global plan of action and a global budget. For comprehensive assignments, which are usually awarded to large consultancies, the 'proposals' can be voluminous documents in which the consultancies use all their expertise to present themselves as the best candidate.

The consultants, who still value a precisely defined contract, will include an orientation phase in their proposal, to be financed by the customer. In practice, this means they incorporate a certain degree of flexibility into their action plan that will enable them to modify the assignment based on their initial experiences, often with consequences for the budget. Experienced customers accept this as they realize that good quality can pay for itself in the end. An unsuccessful consultancy project can lead to the wrong decisions, which is frequently detrimental to the career of the manager who hired the consultant in the first place.

The principal values customized work

Extensive scrutiny of the organization, as proposed in the TSP, is aimed at designing a tailor-made consultancy process. The orientational interviews enable the consultant to learn how people in the organization think, what their views on the problem are and who will be prepared to invest time in the change process. Based on observations of this nature, the consultant designs a tailor-made plan of action, chooses the most suitable role and puts forward a proposal for a feasible result.

Not all consultancy assignments require this level of care and customization. There are various types of assignment in which a certain degree of standardization is possible – for example, when the consultant has a more or less standard consultancy task and the customer has a problem that can be solved using this standard procedure. Examples of standard consultancy tasks are:

- Personnel recruitment (head-hunting)
- Outplacement (finding jobs for personnel elsewhere)
- Partner search (looking for a candidate for a merger or acquisition)
- Market research
- Standard business diagnosis.

Consultancy tasks of this sort often have a fixed price that is not always based on the customary formula of the number of hours multiplied by the hourly rate. This also includes the 'no cure, no pay' contracts, as they are known, as in cases of this sort the intended end result is often easy to measure.

In the list given above, market research and standard diagnosis differ slightly from the other items. They relate to an activity rather than promising a specific result, and their outcome is uncertain. In investigations of this type, both of which also exist in customized forms, the standardization takes the form of a predetermined investigation programme that is carried out for a predetermined price.

In recent decades, there has been a substantial increase in the use of standard diagnoses, mainly due to:

- The efforts made by consultancies to gain more assignments from small and medium-sized businesses. Consultancy work is generally regarded as expensive and abstruse, and standardization makes it easier to understand and accessible for smaller businesses.
- The increasing competition in the consultancy market, which makes it necessary for consultancies to profile themselves using a distinctive consultancy task product. This also explains the creative and catchy names the various consultancy tasks products are often given.
- The tendency for consultants to be called in not only to help solve problems, but also to help prevent problems. This has led to a wide range of preventive business diagnoses being offered. Preventive diagnoses are ideally suited to a programme-directed rather than a problem-directed consultancy process. If a consultant is hired to help track down potential problems and suggest possible areas for improvement, then the most obvious choice is a predetermined inspection programme directed at analysing the primary business activities.

There is now a wide range of business diagnoses on sale in the market. There are diagnostic methods that require a consultant, and there are also courses, workshops and manuals that enable companies to carry out the analysis themselves. An important point when using a standard business diagnosis is that it often contains an implicit vision of what constitutes good business operation. A businessman who hires a consultant for a preventive diagnosis first needs to enquire about his vision or reference model and decide whether this matches up with his own requirements. Many diagnostic consultants cannot make their vision explicit. The questions they use for the diagnosis are based on their own experience and intuition. For example, a diagnosis may assume that a healthy company will be one of the leaders in product innovation, while it is not uncommon for companies to deliberately choose to be followers in the market. Alternatively, it may use low stock levels as a benchmark, while some companies will deliberately choose to maintain a short delivery time, making slightly higher stock levels necessary.

This means that consultants can never apply standard formulae indiscriminately. They must always examine with the customer whether the assumptions inherent in the method match up with the customer's vision of the company and which vital business processes should be focused on. This discussion can lead a consultant to modify the process for this specific case; it can also prompt customers to rethink their business philosophy.

The principal requires supervision of the implementation

The TSP is based on consultancy assignments in which the principal welcomes the attention and involvement of the consultant during the implementation of the recommendations made. This explains the focus on building up support, drawing up a results-directed contract, making use of internal work groups and developing an implementation plan.

However, not all customers welcome this. Some feel confident enough to carry out the implementation themselves. They require consultants because of their independence and authority, based on knowledge and experience, to support a management decision. How this decision is subsequently taken and implemented is the responsibility of the organization itself.

In this case, the consultant is forced into the role of expert. An assignment of this type does not relieve consultants of the obligation to pay implicit attention to the feasibility of their recommendations during their work. After all, a high-quality recommendation that is not followed by the customer is still a failed project. To illustrate this, it is a good idea to look back at Case 1.1.

The principal and consultant decide on the working programme together

The comprehensive intake process in the orientation phase of the TSP finally leads to a plan of action that reflects both the wishes and capabilities of the customer and the expertise of the consultant. The consultant generally sets the tone, having more research experience, but the principal's influence is usually evident. A certain level of input from the principal is actually desirable, both for monitoring the costs and for indicating how far the organization can be stretched.

The opposite situation sometimes arises, particularly in the case of internal consultants, and the customer has the strongest voice in determining the consultancy process. Sometimes a consultant is merely put at the disposal of the customer/manager for a specified period to carry out a number of investigations to be decided on by the customer. Naturally, in these circumstances consultants can contribute their own ideas to the plan of action for each consultancy project, but they are still more follower than leader.

What the internal consultant must always strive for is to acquire and maintain a sufficiently independent position. There is always a risk – partly due to the nature of the contracting – that the consultant will be regarded as a supporter of an existing way of thinking in the organization. So it requires extra effort to be accepted as an objective adviser by all parties. The TSP can be of assistance here. By making contact in advance with all the people involved through orientational interviews, the image of an independent consultant who is not bound by any existing alliance can be reinforced.

Conclusion

In practice, there are many further variations on the situation assumed in the TSP. Our aim was merely to describe a few common examples. It is clear that there may be reasons for deviating from the TSP when designing a consultancy process, but even then it is nearly always possible to adhere to the main principles of the TSP. Even in the case of personnel recruitment, it is important to take note of the current wishes and expectations of the organization in order to facilitate the appointment of the correct candidate. Likewise, a perspective study of a potential bankruptcy case should not be carried out in isolation from the organization.

Support, involvement, feasibility, focus on results, harmonization with external developments and a manageable project approach are the foundations of every effective consultancy process. The way attention is paid to these aspects can differ between consultancy processes depending on the nature of the assignment or the professional views of the consultant involved. In the TSP, these aspects are firmly rooted in a structured working procedure. This helps inexperienced consultants to avoid losing their way amid the numerous events that demand attention during a consultancy project.

References

Argyris, C. and Schön, D.A. (1996). *Organizational Learning: A Theory of Action Perspective*. Reading, MA: Addison-Wesley.

Barcus, S.W. and Wilkinson, J.W. (eds) (1996). *Handbook of Management Consulting Services*. New York: McGraw-Hill.

Bell, C.R. (1986). Entry is a critical phase in consulting. *Journal of Management Consulting*, **3**(1), 4–10.

Biech, E. (1999). *The Business of Consulting, The Basics and Beyond*. San Francisco: Jossey-Bass.

Block, P. (1999). *Flawless Consulting: A Guide to Getting your Expertise Used*. Jossey-Bass Wiley.

Brassard, M. and Ritter, D. (1994). *The Memory Jogger II, A Pocket Guide of Tools for Continuous Improvement & Effective Planning*. Goal/QPC, Methuen (MA).

Chambers, A. and Rand, G. (1997). *Auditing Business Processes (Operational Auditing Handbook)*. New York: Wiley.

Champion, D.P., Kiel, D.H. and McLendon, J.A. (1990). Choosing a consulting role. *Training and Development Journal*, **44**(2), 66–70.

Crossan, M.M., Lame, H.W. and White, R.E. (1999). An organizational learning framework: from intuition to institution. *Academy of Management Review*, **24**(3), 522–37.

Dillman, D.A. (2000). *Mail and Internet Surveys, The Tailored Design Method*. New York: Wiley.

Emans, B. (2004). *Interviewing: Theory, Techniques and Training*. Groningen: Stenfert Kroese.

Emden, J. and Becker, L. (2004). *Presentation Skills for Students*. Basingstoke: Palgrave-MacMillan.

Fink, A. (1995a). *How to Design Surveys*. London: Sage.

Fink, A. (1995b). *How to Sample in Surveys*. London: Sage.

Fink, A. (1995c). *How to Report on Surveys*. London: Sage.

Greiner, L.E. and Metzger, R.O. (1983). *Consulting to Management*. Englewood Cliffs, NJ: Prentice-Hall.

Greiner, L.E. and Poulfelt, F. (2004). *Handbook of Management Consulting: The Contemporary Consultant*. Mason, OH: South-Western.

Grit, R. (2003). *Project Management*. Groningen: Wolters-Noordhoff.

Gundry, L.K. and Buchko, A.A. (1996). *Field Casework, Methods for Consulting to Small and Startup Businesses.* London: Sage.

Hale, J. (1998). *The Performance Consultant's Fieldbook, Tools and Techniques for Improving Organizations and People.* San Francisco: Jossey-Bass.

Harvey, D.F. and Brown, D.R. (2005). *An Experiential Approach to Organization Development.* Englewood Cliffs, NJ: Prentice-Hall.

Hatch, M.J. (1997). *Organization Theory, Modern, Symbolic and Post Modern Perspectives.* Oxford: Oxford University Press.

Hofstede, G. (1994). *Cultures and Organizations: Software of the Mind.* Profile Business.

Jankowicz, A.D. (2000). *Business Research Projects.* Thomson.

Kaplan, R.S. and Norton, D.P. (1996). *The Balanced Score Card, Translating Strategy into Action.* Cambridge, MA: Harvard Business School Press.

Katz, D. and Kahn, R.L. (1978). *The Social Psychology of Organizations,* 2nd edn. New York: Wiley.

Kelly, R.E. (1986). *Consulting: The Complete Guide to a Profitable Career.* New York: Charles Scribner.

Kerzner, H. (2003). *Project Management: A Systems Approach to Planning, Scheduling and Controlling.* New York: Wiley.

Kubr, M. (2002). *Management Consulting: A Guide to the Profession.* Geneva: International Labour Office.

Lewin, M.D. (1995). *The Overnight Consultant.* New York: Wiley.

Lippitt, G. and Lippitt, R. (1994). *The Consulting Process in Action.* San Francisco: Jossey-Bass.

Lockyer, K.G. and Gordon, J.H. (1991). *Critical Path Analysis and Other Project Network Techniques.* London: Pitman.

Majchrzak, A., Cooper, L.P. and Neece, O.E. (2004). Knowledge reuse for innovation. *Management Science,* **50**(2), 174–89.

Mandel, S. (2000). *Effective Presentation Skills: A Practical Guide for Better Speaking.* Menlo Park, CA: Crisp Publications.

Margerison, C.J. (1996). *Managerial Consulting Skills: A Practical Guide.* Aldershot: Gower.

Martin, P.E. *et al.* (1986). *Project Management Memory Jogger.* Goal/QPC, Methuen (MA).

Moorman, C and Miner, A.S. (1997). The impact of organizational memory on new product performance and creativity. *Journal of Marketing Research,* **24**(Feb), 91–106.

Morgan, G. (1986). *Images of Organization.* London: Sage.

Nees, D.B. and Greiner, L.E. (1985). Seeing behind the look-alike management consultants. *Organizational Dynamics,* Winter.

Overholt, M.H. and Altier, W.J. (1988). Participative process consulting: the hard and soft of it. *Journal of Management Consulting,* **4**(3), 13–24.

Saunders, M.N.K. (2002). *Research Methods for Business Students.* Englewood Cliffs, NJ: Prentice-Hall.

Schaffer, R.H. (2002). *High Impact Consulting.* San Francisco: Jossey-Bass.

Schaffer, R.H. and Michaelson, K.E. (1989). The incremental strategy for consulting success. *Journal of Management Consulting,* **5**(2), 8–14.

Schaffer, R.H. and Thomson, H.A. (1992). Successful change programs begin with results. *Harvard Business Review,* Jan/Feb, 21–31.

Schein, E.H. (1999). *Process Consultation Revisited, Building the Helping Relationship*. Reading, MA: Addison-Wesley.

Swieringa, J. and Wierdsma, A.F.M. (1992). *Building a Learning Organization*. Reading, MA: Addison-Wesley.

Tjosvold, D. (1991). *The Conflict-positive Organization: Stimulate Diversity and Create Unity*. Reading, MA: Addison-Wesley.

Turner, A.N. (1982). Consulting is more than giving advice. *Harvard Business Review*, **60**(5), 26–35.

Turner, J.R. (1998). *Handbook of Project-based Management: Improving the Process for Achieving Strategic Objectives*. New York: McGraw-Hill.

Van Aken, J.E. (2004). Management research based on the paradigm of the design sciences: the quest for tested and grounded technological rules. *Journal of Management Studies*, **41**(2), 219–46.

Van Strien, P.J. (1997). Towards a methodology of psychological practice. *Theory and Psychology*, **7**(5), 683–700.

Van Tuijl, H.F.J.M. (1997).Critical success factors in developing ProMES: will the end result be an accepted control loop? *Leadership and Organization Development Journal*, **18**(7), 346–54.

Wickam, P.A. (2004). *Management Consulting: Delivering an Effective Project*. Harlow: Prentice-Hall.

Williams, A.P.O. and Woodward, S. (1994). *The Competitive Consultant: A Client-oriented Approach for Achieving Superior Performance*. Basingstoke: Macmillan.

Index

DATE DUE

HD
30.4
.K444
2006

Keizer, Jimme.

Business research projects